1 MONTH OF FREE READING

at

www.ForgottenBooks.com

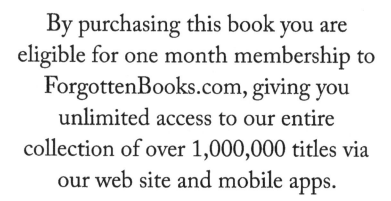

By purchasing this book you are eligible for one month membership to ForgottenBooks.com, giving you unlimited access to our entire collection of over 1,000,000 titles via our web site and mobile apps.

To claim your free month visit:

www.forgottenbooks.com/free505207

ISBN 978-0-267-54399-1
PIBN 10505207

This book is a reproduction of an important historical work. Forgotten Books uses
state-of-the-art technology to digitally reconstruct the work, preserving the original format
whilst repairing imperfections present in the aged copy. In rare cases, an imperfection in
the original, such as a blemish or missing page, may be replicated in our edition. We do,
however, repair the vast majority of imperfections successfully; any imperfections that
remain are intentionally left to preserve the state of such historical works.

Historical Address

DELIVERED BY

Rev. EDWARD A. CHASE

AT THE

Centennial Celebration

OF THE

Congregational Church

HAMPDEN, MASS.

— ——

November 18, 1885

Historical Address

DELIVERED BY

Rev. EDWARD A. CHASE

AT THE

Centennial Celebration

OF THE

Congregational Church

HAMPDEN, MASS.

November 18, 1885

HARTFORD, CONN.

Press of The Case, Lockwood & Brainard Company

1898

PREFATORY NOTE.

IT becomes my duty and my pleasure to acknowledge my obligation to those who have helped furnish materials for this address. Particularly am I indebted to the "History of Wilbraham," by Dr. Stebbins, for the earlier portions of the town history; also to Mr. Jonathan F. Morris of Hartford, Conn., for facts bearing upon the earlier days of the parish. The obligation extends to the pages of *The Religious Intelligencer*, vol. 7, for a large share of the account of the revival under Mr. Nettleton. I should have been glad always to have indicated their help by quotation marks on the page, had it not been that my own researches were so intermingled as to render it not always possible so to do. It has seemed better to acknowledge the debt in this place once and for all.

EDWARD A. CHASE.

IT was the desire and expectation of many at the time when the address of Mr. Chase was given that it would soon be published. The publication, however, was delayed for the purpose of gathering the other addresses made on that occasion, some of which contained very interesting reminiscences. The collection of those addresses failed, and time has gone on without any further attempt to obtain them. After the lapse of so many years the publishers interested in the history of the church of their fathers, and believing that there was much in the address worthy of preservation, have ventured to publish it, the manuscript having come into the possession of Mr. West. Some notes have been added containing matter which did not come within the knowledge or reach of Mr. Chase.

Brief genealogies of the families connected with the church when Mr. Warren was ordained, have also been added so far as they could be obtained.

JOHN WEST,

JONATHAN F. MORRIS.

Springfield and Hartford,
   March, 1898.

THE movement for the centennial of the Congregational Church in Hampden, which was celebrated November 18, 1885, was begun in the month of January previous. The centennial exercises held in the church began at 10 o'clock, A. M. The church was tastefully ornamented for the occasion, with plants and evergreen. Dr. George T. Ballard was president of the day. The exercises began with a selection by the choir, after which came prayer and reading of the scriptures. A hymn was sung by the whole congregation, following which Deacon A. B. Newell made a brief address of welcome. The programme was as follows:

1785   1885

FIRST CONGREGATIONAL CHURCH

OF HAMPDEN.

ONE HUNDRETH ANNIVERSARY,

WEDNESDAY, NOVEMBER 18,

At 10 o'clock, A. M.

1785   1885

ORDER OF EXERCISES.

WEDNESDAY MORNING.

- I. MUSIC — 10 o'clock, A. M.
- II. READING OF SCRIPTURES.
- III. PRAYER.
- IV. HYMN.
- V. ADDRESS OF WELCOME.
- VI. HYMN.
- VII. HISTORICAL ADDRESS.
- VIII. HYMN.

Intermission and Collation.

WEDNESDAY AFTERNOON.

- I. MUSIC.
- II. ADDRESSES BY FORMER PASTORS.
- III. HYMN.
- IV. ADDRESSES BY INVITED GUESTS.
- V. HYMN.
- VI. CELEBRATION OF THE LORD'S SUPPER.
- VII. BENEDICTION.

Social Reunion in the Evening.

HISTORICAL ADDRESS.

It is strange how life destroys some of our ideas.

I had been wont to think of youth as a time for looking into the future rather than into the past; a time of imagination rather than for the discussion of plain everyday facts,— and yet I find myself to-day placed to recall for you the events of the past century of your church life; surely the theme demands a longer memory, a better judgment, a readier pen than mine,—yet that which I have I gladly bring to your service.

The day is one of thanksgiving and congratulation. Thanks to God, who, by His wisdom, has directed the church through the eventful century; thanks to Him as the faithful promisor, who, in all this time, has fulfilled his word for the field, and thereby has sustained the life of the people; thanks to Him as the loving Father who has crowned our homes with their love and precious sympathy.

A day of congratulation to you, for your steadfast faith and that of your fathers,

> "Men whose hands were brown with toil,
> Who backed by no ancestral graves,
> Hewed down the wood and tilled the soil ;
> And thereby won a prouder fame,
> Than follows a king's or a warrior's name,"

men who, in the scantiness of their profit, found enough for themselves and the Lord, too, and by their noble work made possible the blessings of to-day.

The chief value of such historic looking back is, I conceive, to get motive for future work. It is true in our daily lives, whatever be their specific labor, that yesterday conditions to-day, and to-day to-morrow, in its wisdom and efficiency of toil. So is it in our church life; the successes of the past, and the failures as well, may be to us wise instructors. And these very successes make it the more incumbent on us that we do well for the Master.

I like the saying of our statesman that "life is neither
pain nor pleasure, but serious business, to be entered upon with
courage and ended with the spirit of self-sacrifice." And I
would make that "serious business," cost what it may, the
establishing of the kingdom of Christ in the world — which
your fathers sought to do, in their own hearts first, and then
in the hearts of their fellows. Their work has now fallen to
us,— God give us to do it well.

Let us come, then, to our subject to-day with a feeling of
real gratitude to God; of rejoicing in the success attained; and
with the desire to get wisdom and renewed courage for the toil
of the future.

The historian of the town of Wilbraham has so fully told
the story of its civic life that a detailed account of its early
days becomes unnecessary on my part. Yet because the civic
and the church life of those first years are inextricably inter-
woven, and to the end that the address of to-day may have a
completeness of its own, it becomes unavoidable to walk in
paths already trodden, and to say as briefly as the best under-
standing of the history permits, some things not unfamiliar
to you.

In the seventeenth century the town of Springfield included territory from the mountains on her north to the south
line of the present Enfield, and from Russell on the west to
Monson on the east.

Of course, all this territory was not inhabited, part of it
had not even been appropriated to the inhabitants of Springfield. This unappropriated land, a part of which lay on the
east and a part on the west of the Connecticut River, was
known as the "Outward Commons." When Andros, governor of Massachusetts, threatened to take away the charter of
the colony, in order that these commons might not revert to
the crown of England, the town of Springfield voted to make
the land the property of its individual inhabitants. A certain
amount was reserved for the ministry and schools, and the rest
was alloted in the following way: all the land was divided into
five sections: each of the legal citizens, including one " Glover
the teacher," received some part of all five sections, the propor-
tion of each being according to the value of his estate and the
number of his male children. It was found that when the
land was surveyed in 1729 only sixteen feet were allowed to

the rod, so that on the south side of the third division there remained unappropriated a strip of land sixty-two rods wide and four miles long. This received the name of " overplus land." It was within the limits of our present town, and became the farm of the man who built the frame of the first meeting-house, whose name will appear later on.

Of these " outward commons " thus alloted, the third section and a large part of the second, with their " overplus " land, became afterwards the town of Wilbraham, of which, until recently, we have been the South Parish.

The real history of Wilbraham commenced in the North Parish, afterwards so called, ten years before our own. It began with Nathaniel Hitchcock, who settled in 1730, followed within the next four years by Noah Alford, Daniel Warner, and Nathaniel Warriner.

At the close of ten years the settlement consisted of twenty-six families, living in houses framed but " poorly finished, scantily glazed, and meagerly furnished." Their business was farming, their toil was severe, their hardships and inconveniences a great many, but their reward large enough to make them persevere.

In the year 1741 the " outward commons " were incorporated into the Fourth Parish of Springfield for the support of a minister. In this year, in the spring, the South Parish, afterwards so called, began its history by the coming of one Stephen Stebbins from Longmeadow. He settled near the north bank of the Scantic, where Mr. Mortimer Pease now lives. The house he built was moved nearly a century ago, and now is used as a barn on the place owned by Mrs. Pliny Allen, and used as a hotel. Some of the boards of that house may be seen on the north side of the barn to-day. Aaron Stebbins, his brother, built north of him, on the place where Mr. Wall now resides, just north of the schoolhouse. Paul Langdon, who brought the first four-wheeled wagon into the place, in which he moved his worldly goods from Salem to Hopkinton, from there to Union, and from Union to South Wilbraham, settled south of Stephen Stebbins, on the farm now occupied by Edward Bartlett. This farm was the " overplus " land of which mention was made, and Mr. Langdon obtained it through the aid of Mr. Pynchon, by getting those whose farms lay adjacent to it to sign off any right they might

2

claim in it.   Abner Chapin from Chicopee settled south of the
Scantic, where Silas Chapin and the widow of Ralph S. Chapin
now reside, the farms being separated by the road.

Lewis Langdon, son of Paul, built the first sawmill in town
in 1750.   It stood on the south side of the present road, a little
east of Ravine Mill, and some remains of its timbers are yet
to be seen.

Another early settler was William King, who built on the
spot on which this present church stands.   His was a lean-to
house, the back running to the ground.   It afterwards passed
into the hands of Robert Sessions, and the old frame is, I suppose, that of the house occupied by Mr. Whittaker, the second
below the church.

William Stacy from Salem settled on the mountain south
of the Scantic, where Albert Lee now resides; Moses Stebbins
where S. T. Ballard now lives; Comfort Chaffee on the place
afterwards owned by William Chaffee, where Homer Lee now
resides.   There was also Jabez Hendrick, who settled on the
place now owned by John Whittaker, a house now unoccupied,
situated off in the fields.   Upon the hills was Daniel Carpenter, where James L. Weeks now lives, and besides these,
Henry Badger, Isaac Morris, Rowland Crocker, Benjamin
Skinner, and Ezekiel Russell, the last named settling where
Daniel Flynn now lives.

We see that many of the first settlers kept along the line
of the water, and so we may suppose that as the settlement
grew it increased along the line of what is now the main street
of the village.   The same thing occurred in the south part of
the town that had taken place in the north; as the inhabitants
increased they felt the desire to have a preaching service in
their own midst.   It was a long way to the meeting-house, the
roads were poor, the means of conveyance not the most comfortable.   We, therefore, find that in 1765, twenty-four years
after the coming of Stephen Stebbins, the people here asked
the town for money to support preaching during the winter;
this was refused.   Their next move was in 1767, when they
endeavored to gain at town meeting, in December, the privilege
of having preaching during " two months in the Winter season
upon their own cost "; this was also denied them.   But
whether in this offer to pay for their own preaching the people
here desired to be let off from their tithes at the north meeting-

house I am not able to find out. The people were not willing
to be denied their request, and in order to accomplish their object, five years later they asked to be made a separate town.
* Note " A." This did not work, either, until, in 1778, after
several adjourned meetings, it was voted to divide the town
into two parishes. This vote was reconsidered, but in 1780
the people made an appeal to be a separate parish on both town
and general court. In 1781, at the town meeting of December 24th, a committee from out of town was chosen to consider
the method of dividing the town into parishes. This committee consisted of John Hale, Luke Bliss, and William Pynchon,
Jr. They rendered their report, dated Springfield, February
21, 1782. It was as follows:

" We have taken into our deliberate consideration the
several matters you, by your committee, thought fit to lay before us, which has brought us to a determination that some
division of your town is necessary, concerning the manner of
which you have been pleased to refer yourselves to us for aid
and advice. Our opinion you have in the following report.
The committee consider it a great unhappiness that a town so
respectable as the town of Wilbraham is should, in the management of their publick affairs, suffer such animosities to arise
amongst them as to have any tendency to prevent the general
benefits and advantages that might otherwise arise to them, by
inculcating those generous sentiments of love and esteem,
which is so essential to the well-being of every society.
Whether by the local. situation of the inhabitants of the
several parts of said town, or whether by the real or supposed
indiscretion of any persons, in the amicable management of
your publick affairs make it expedient that a Division should
take place amongst us, we pretend not to say.

" Though the manner of it seems only to be referred to us,
yet we conceive it may not be improper for us to declare our
concurrance in sentiment with you, that some division is become necessary: Touching the mode of it and how it shall be
made—It is the united opinion of the committee and which
they conceive will best accommodate the inhabitants of the
several parts of the town, that it be divided into two parishes,
by the name of the North and South Parishes, by a line coinciding with the south line of the lot whereon Nathaniel Bliss
deceased lived, from the westward bound of said town to the

Monson line: — (with this exception) that the inhabitants of said town living on the west from the top of the mountain to the south side of Lieut. Thomas Merrick's lot to the westward bounds of said town with their estates, be annexed to the North Parish and that the inhabitants living east from the top of the mountain from the said south side of sd Bliss's lot north to the south side of Lot originally laid out to Jonathan Taylors estate to Monson line, be annexed to the south parish with their estates, if each or any of said inhabitants should choose so to do — they making their choice previous to said parish being incorporated, and they thus choosing to be annexed to the respective Parishes forever.

" And that each part of said town have and enjoy equal parts of the land sequestered for the use of the ministry, or monies or securities for money that may be in the treasury — the proceeds of the sale of said lands or any other money or security for money or donation for the support of the gospel, be and remain to each parish in equal parts.

" And the Meeting house standing in the north part of said town be and belong to the north parish so long as they continue to meet in it for the publick worship of God.

" Should that love and union take place which your committee earnestly recommend and which is so essentially to the well being of every society, they are of opinion that said house be and remain for the use of the whole of said town for the purpose of carrying on their meeting in future.

" We sincerely wish that love and harmony may again take place amongst you, that we may have the satisfaction of knowing that our poor endeavors have in some measure contributed toward the effecting an event so important.

" We are, gentlemen, with sentiments of love and esteem, your friends and humble servants."

In accord with this report of advice a committee of the town was chosen, and over the signatures of Moses Stebbins, Enoch Burt, and Philip Lyon, this petition was sent to the Legislature:

COMMONWEALTH OF MASSACHUSETTS.

" To the Honorable Senate & House of Representatives in General Court Assembled—

" The petition of the inhabitants of Wilbraham — Humbly sheweth — That whereas it is of great importance that we constantly attend upon the preaching of the gospel, and as by the annexing of Wales to the south part of said town the present meeting-house is much out of the center, and by the blessing of heaven we are so multiplied that the attendance upon the preaching of the gospel is rendered very difficult, and almost impossible for great numbers, to attend on a preached gospel and whereas there is at present no settled minister in said town and as the wants of a division of said town, will probably if not inevitably prevent the settlement of one, to the real hurt of said town—We are humbly of opinion that it is an opportune season to have said town divided — and as we hope we are able to support two ministers and as nature has seemed to form us for two parishes being near nine miles north and south, and four miles and a half east and west — We the subscribers therefore (in behalf of this town) Petition by the name of the North and South Parishes your honors to incorporate this town into two parishes — by a line coinciding with the south line of the lot whereon Nathaniel Bliss deceased lived, from the westward bounds of said town to the Monson line: — (with this exception) that the inhabitants of said town living on the west from the top of the mountain to the south side of Lieut. Thos. Merricks lot to the westward bounds of said town with their estates be annexed to the north parish and that the inhabitants living on the east from the top of the mountain from said south side of said Bliss's lot north to the south side of the lot originally laid out to Jonathan Taylor's estate to Monson line be annexed to the South Parish with their estates, if each or any of said inhabitants should choose so to do — They making their choice previous to said parish being incorporated, and they thus choosing, to be annexed to the respective parishes forever —

" And that each part of said town have and enjoy equal parts of the land sequestered for the use of the ministry, or the money or for securities for money that may be in the Treasury, the proceeds of the sale of said land or any other money or security for money or donation for the support of the gospel, be and remain to each parish in equal parts. And the meeting-house standing in the North part of said town be and belong to the north parish so long as they continue to meet in it for the publick worship of God.

" This petition for the substance of it is agreeable to a report of a committee unanimously chosen by this town . . . to advise this town in what manner to be divided, which report was accepted by a vote of the town at a legal town meeting, April 5, 1782 — and at the same meeting we the subscribers were chosen a committee to refer the above Petition to your honors to take into serious consideration and act thereupon as you in your wisdom shall think best — as in duty bound we ever pray.

"P. S. We pray your honors to annex Lt. Thomas Merrick with his estate to the North Parish, he having made his choice so to be. Also Mr. David Wood to the South Parish with his estate He having likewise made his choice so to be. Or any other of said inhabitants included in said committee's report, they signifying their choice to your honors before the incorporation of said parishes."

The petition was granted and an act of incorporation issued June 20, 1782. It ran as follows:

"Commonwealth of Massachusetts. In the year of our Lord one thousand seven hundred and eighty-two. An act for dividing the town of Wilbraham into two separate parishes.

"Whereas for the greater convenience of attending the publick worship of God, it is found necessary to divide the town of Wilbraham into two separate parishes, be it enacted by the Senate and House of Representatives in general Court assembled and by the authority òf the same that the said town of Wilbraham be and the same is hereby divided into two separate parishes by the names of the North Parish and the South Parish by a line coinciding with the south of the lot whereon Nathaniell Bliss deceased lately lived, from the west bounds of said town to Monson line — and the said parishes above mentioned and each of them be and hereby are severally invested with all the powers rights and privileges which parishes in this commonwealth are by law invested with — and be it further enacted by the authority aforesaid that Mr. Thomas Merrick with his lands and estates be and hereby is annexed to the North Parish above mentioned and David Wood, Jesse Carpenter and Jonah Beebe with their lands and other estates be and they hereby are annexed to the South Parish in the said town, anything in this act to the contrary notwithstanding — And be it further enacted that each of the parishes aforesaid shall have and enjoy in equal shares the lands heretofore sequestered devised or given for the use or support of the ministry and the monies or securities for money that may be in the treasury, and as well the proceeds of the sale of lands, as any other monies or securities for money that have been given to the inhabitants of the said town for the support of the gospel. And be it further enacted — that the inhabitants of the North Parish aforesaid shall have a right to improve the meeting house now standing in the said parish for the purpose of Public Worship so long as they shall think proper so to improve it.

" And be it further enacted that John Bliss Esq. be and hereby is empowered to issue his warrants to some principal inhabitants of each of the said parishes requiring them to warn the inhabitants of the parishes to which they respectively belong to meet at such time and place in each of the said parishes as by such warrants shall be duly specified and then choose such officers as may be necessary to manage the affairs of the said parishes. And the inhabitants qualified by law to vote being so assembled shall be and hereby are impowered to choose such officers in their respective parishes accordingly."

Now that they had gained the desired end, what means had they to support preaching? In 1780, January 10th, Nathaniel Warriner, a deacon of the old church, died. Having no children, he gave by his will four hundred pounds, " To be the one-half given to the support of a gospel ministry, provided that all other churches which are or may be in this town of a different constitution from the standing order of churches in this land shall forever be excluded from receiving any benefit from the same."

By the act which divided the town, as we have seen, each of the parishes was to have and enjoy in equal shares the monies or securities for money given to the inhabitants for the support of the gospel. The gift of Mr. Warriner and other funds were, therefore, divided, and seven hundred and fifty dollars was given to this South Parish.

On the green yonder, in those early days, stood some large oak trees, and under those trees the first preaching was held. In cold weather the services were conducted in private houses. The frame of the first meeting-house was built by Paul Langdon, and was raised in June, 1783. The building stood on the green and faced to the west. It was but a poor affair, yet was it none the less the House of God, the rallying point of the people, their place of spiritual comfort.

They tell us that for many years it was unpainted, with no pews, but only rough boards for seats, and a rude box for a pulpit. The timbers of the walls and roof were all exposed, and became the nesting places of birds.

The first parish treasurer was Colonel Bliss, who served from 1782 till 1784, when he was succeeded by David Burt. *

On March 12, 1784, the parish was assessed £50 13s. 6d. for hiring preaching. * Note " B." August 2, 1784, the parish committee drew an order on Treasurer Burt for £6 6s. in favor of Capt. Paul Langdon and Lieut. Samuel Sexton, " to enable them to pay Mr. Smith, for preaching with us last winter." March 28, 1785, it was voted to Capt. Paul Langdon 8s. 6d. " for going to Westford after Rev. Mr. Hutchinson." It was in this year, 1785, that the church was organized. It is strange, indeed, that no record of the month or day remains; but the most careful search has failed to reveal it. What ministers helped in its organization we do not know; there was at the time no minister in the north parish, for Mr. Merrick was dead and Mr. Willard was not called until 1787.

Fortunately, the " Form of Union " under which the people bound themselves together has been preserved to us — copied by the first pastor into the book kept by him, from some records (as I suppose) accessible to him, but now lost. It reads as follows:

" We the subscribers, do hereby covenant with God and each other as a particular visible church of Christ, to be come organized by this act and to enjoy all the ordinances of worship and discipline, which our Lord Jesus Christ hath appointed to have observed in his church to the end of the world. We give up ourselves to the Lord Jehovah, the one only living and true God, subsisting in three persons, Father, Son and Holy Ghost, equal in power and glory. We solemnly avouch the Lord Jehovah to be our God and the God of our children, and agreeable to this covenant we dedicate them to God in baptism, and engage to bring them up in the nurture and admonition of the Lord.

---

* Stephen West succeeded Mr. Burt.

" We believe that the scriptures of the Old and new testaments are the word of God and that they are our only rule of faith and practice.

" We bind ourselves by this covenant to observe the special ordinances of the New Testament, the sacraments of baptism and the Lord's supper, and all the other commands and ordinances of the Lord revealed to us in His holy word and to submit ourselves to the government and discipline of Christ in his church.

" We give up ourselves to one another in the Lord firmly covenanting and binding ourselves to walk together as a Congregational church of Christ, and resolve by divine grace assisting to walk worthy of the vocation wherewith we are called, with all lowliness and meekness, with long suffering, forbearing one another in love, endeavoring to keep the unity of the spirit in the bond of peace.

" And whereas our great redeemer hath by His ascension, among other gifts, purchased and given that of pastors and teachers for the perfecting of the saints, for the work of the ministry, and for the edifying of the body of Christ,— we engage to aid and stand by an orthodox and regular and Godly ministry, which may at any time be set over us, according to our place and power, and with their joint concurrence will uphold the impartial administration of all Gods Holy Ordinances in this church.

" Finally, we desire to maintain a constant sense of our manifold unworthiness of the great privileges and blessing of the Covenant of Grace, to walk humbly with God and fervently to supplicate His Gracious Presence with us.

" That the God of peace who brought again from the dead our Lord Jesus Christ that great shepherd of the sheep through the blood of the everlasting covenant may make us perfect in every good work to do His will, working in us that which is well pleasing in his sight through Jesus Christ to whom be glory forever and ever, Amen."

From its organization in 1785 until the call of Mr. Warren, the church was supplied by different ministers. Among the papers of Mr. Bliss it is recorded that on May 1, 1786, Enoch Burt and Moses Stebbins, Jr., " ministerial committee," certified to the parish committee that they had employed Mr. Abishai Colton " candidate preacher to preach with us a fast and four sabbaths at four dollars per day amounting in the whole to Six£." March 28, 1786, the parish voted 6s. to Capt. Paul Langdon and Lieut. Samuel Sexton " for carrying grains to Springfield in pay for preaching." April 9, 1786, 3s. were voted to Saml. Sexton " for going after preacher." November 10, 1786, the parish voted £10 "for glazing the lower part of the meeting house, also 20£ to hire preaching." April 9, 1787, Moses Stebbins, Jr., was voted 9s. 5d. " for going after preacher," and to Saml. Sexton 3s. for the same purpose. November 30, 1787, the parish voted £20 " to hire preaching." January 15, 1788, Saml. Sexton, Enoch Burt, and Moses Stebbins, Jr., " ministerial committee," certified to the committee and assessor of the parish that they had hired preaching, namely, Mr. Ebenezer Kingsbury two sabbaths, Mr. Lathrop Thompson ten sabbaths, at £1 5s. per sabbath, amounting to £14 8s. March 12, 1788, the ministerial committee certified that " Moses Stebbins, Jr., had paid Mr. Thompson for preaching £1. 2s.," which he should be paid out of the parish treasury. This is the last record we have before the coming of Mr. Warren.

Here then ends our first period. It has been one of intense effort. In it the sturdy pioneer has broken the fields; has felled the trees of the forest; has built himself the mill whereby to saw the boards to build his house and barn; has asserted his independence, his determination to have and protect his own rights; has built for himself a fane of prayer, wherein he has worshiped the God whom he believes the maker and guide of his life.

Herein the history of the South Parish has begun, and the home life, the industrial life, and the Church life of the century are foreshadowed.

II.

Now that the people had a meeting-house, a membership of sixty-five, and a fund of money, their next thought was for a settled minister. Near the beginning of the year 1788 a young man preached in the old meeting-house on yonder green. I am not so far away from the starting point but I can myself imagine something of the young man's feeling. Coming, as he did, from a church of longer settlement, the house itself must have strongly impressed him. I do not mean awakened in him a feeling of pride because of the rude surroundings, but, on the contrary, the building with its unfinished walls, its slab seats, its upper unglassed windows, its box pulpit, its roof open in many places to the sky, all this must have made the young man, as he stood to proclaim the word of the Lord, feel the spiritual realness of the God he preached, who, Himself all beautiful and the maker of earth's beauty, could yet be truly worshiped in so unadorned a place, must have made him feel the devotion of this people to their God, because they were determined to have in their midst some house dedicated to His service.

In the front seat, before the preacher, probably sat Enoch Burt and John Hitchcock, for they were the first deacons. Somewhere in the audience would be Colonel John Bliss, a man of affairs; William King, a man of large property; Paul Langdon, an old soldier of the Revolution, now a prominent man in the church and town. The audience was a sturdy one, not to be pleased with anything less than sound truth. The young man seems to have won their favor, for on April 18, 1788, the parish voted " to give Mr. Warren a call to settle with us in the work of the gospel ministry "—in favor of the call 53, against 7.

At the same time it was voted to give Mr. Warren as an encouragement to settle £150; £100 to be paid in one year and the remaining £50 within two years from the time of his settling,— 45 votes in favor with 10 against. They also voted him a salary of £70 yearly, with twenty-four cords of wood each year. Three months after this, on July 14th, the vote was changed in regard to the salary. The parish now decided to " pay Mr. Warren from the time of his settlement to the first Monday in February, 1789, in the following articles,— Wheat, Rye, Indian Corn, Oats, Wool or Flax at the currant market price of those articles at that time; and the one-half of his salary ever after to be paid in the above articles on the first Monday of February of each year at the current market price at the time of payment." The parish further pledged itself, in case Mr. Warren should purchase a settlement, to become obligated " by a committee or by some other way they should adopt " to the person of whom he purchased to the value of £150 as voted on the 18th day of April.

A committee of three — Deacon John Hitchcock, John

Bliss, Esq., and Lieutenant Samuel Sexton — was chosen to acquaint Mr. Warren with the call of the church, the settlement fund, and the salary.

There is no church record of the ordination services. Record remains, however, in the handwriting of Mr. Warren, of the ministers invited, as also his letter accepting the call. Tradition tells where the dinner was held, and a manuscript history of churches has preserved the name of the preacher and the text of the sermon. Using these things, with some personal facts, for our data, for the sake of the picture let us suppose those arrived who were invited, and imagine the council convened. It is called to order, the moderator and scribe chosen, and prayer for God's guidance offered. The doings of the parish are called for, and Moses Stebbins, Jr., the clerk, comes forward and reads the vote which we have already considered. The moderator now asks for Mr. Warren's reply to their offers, and Mr. Stebbins reads this letter:

"To the Church and Society in the South Parish of Wilbraham.

"Brethren and Friends: I have taken into serious consideration the invitation which you gave me to settle with you in the work of the Gospel Ministry. The proceedings of your meetings have been laid before me by your committee. And looking up to heaven for direction I have endeavored impartially to attend to the arguments for and against my settleing. I have considered your circumstances as a union, have attended to the proposals you made for my temporal support; and to the prospect of my being useful among you. Giving all the arguments their just weight, I think at present they preponderate in favor of my settling. And therefore following as far as I know my own heart, the dictates of providence and duty, I now present you with my answer in the affirmative. Should nothing turn up altering the present appearance of things, I am now willing to proceed with you to the necessary steps for ordination.

"Brethren, you must be sensible that the work to which you invite me is great and arduous. You will allow me then earnestly to solicit an interest in your prayers to the great head of the church that should Providence fix me here as your watchman, I may have grace to be faithful and wisdom to be successful. Should such a connection take place, may it serve to promote our mutual happiness here and hereafter, and the advancement of the Redeemer's kingdom.

" All of which with suitable respects is the sincere desire and prayer of him who devotes himself to your service in Christ. MOSES WARREN."

Information as to the young man's education is now desired. Rev. Elisha Fish, his former pastor, is present and vouches for this: that he graduated at Harvard in 1784 and then studied theology with him at Milford, where he was licensed.

The pastor-elect is now called to give some account of his religious experience, and to be questioned on his doctrinal views. He comes forward; a man of about thirty, slight and rather short, fine-grained in feature, dressed in the Continental garb, with long stockings and knee breeches, and wearing black silk gloves.

His testimony is that he was born in Upton, of Worcester County, Massachusetts. His father, Jonas Warren, was a deacon in the church; his mother was also a Christian. He was very early reminded of death and the solemn scenes of an eternal state. These instructions and admonitions made some impression on his mind even in childhood. In his youth he began to seek after God and entertained the hope that he become a subject of regenerating grace; and I shall not go far wrong, I think, learning as I have the belief of the man in God's providential care, if I say he would give as reason for his entering the ministry the real belief that God had called and led him into it. His theological views are those of the New England fathers, and thus meet the approval of the council assembled.

All things being deemed satisfactory, it is decided to ordain Mr. Warren to the ministry and to install him over this church. This was on the 2d of September, for the letter missive called for the council to meet on this date; but the record of his ordination is September 3d. Therefore, I understand that the examination was on one day and the ordination services the next. The council, therefore, now adjourns until the morrow, hospitably entertained meantime by the people; before the cheerful open fires now passing the merry laugh, and now telling in turn of the ways in which God has been leading and blessing them.

The morrow comes and the council and the people meet for the, ordination services. The sermon is preached by Rev. Elisha Fish, Jr., of Windsor, Mass., from the words of Malachi, ii, 7: " For the priest's lips should keep knowledge and they should seek the law at his mouth; for he is the messenger of the Lord of Hosts." The services are finished, and all adjourn for dinner to the house of Colonel Bliss on the hill — the place, though not the house, where Miss Caroline Morris now lives. Tradition says there was not room enough in the fireplace to cook for so many, and so part of the dinner was prepared out of doors under the trees. The first course was of boiled things, then came the roasts, and, I suppose, something in the way of liquor — just to make the turkey a little less dry. At last the dinner with its good cheer is done, the members of the council wish the new pastor God-speed in his work, the people return to their homes, and the young man, still unmarried, is left to lead the people by the counsels of the Lord into the paths of pure thought and life. * Note " G."

It is not an easy life, that of this young minister; there were cases of discipline in the church which produced hard feelings, seeming to be necessary none the less, and which tended all the time to keep the church pure and to make possible the prosperous days that came later on.

The writer of the history of Wilbraham gives in the appendix of his book an account of the case of the discipline of John Williams as one which was very foolish. It is possible that some evidence is available now that did not come to his hand, and also that the standpoint from which one looks may alter opinions. I believe that the church was at fault in her methods, but also that Mr. Williams gave offense, and that both learned a lesson by which they profited. The facts of this discipline will be interesting as a picture of the early church life under Mr. Warren, and their stating necessary to the conclusions reached.

On the 7th of March, 1792, the church met to consult about the case of Mr. John Williams, who was propounded for communion. But the number being small they adjourned to the 14th. On this latter date, " difficulties being so far removed, they voted to invite Mr. Williams to come forward and offer himself to their communion." On the 4th of April the church were desired to stop after the service, at which time

Mr. Williams " voluntarily exhibited a confession for speaking unadvisedly at a certain time and place, ' By George, bring him along.' " He had been accused publicly of profaning the name of God, which he denied he did. The church came to no vote, but chose a committee " to inquire into the difficulty, to obtain what light they could upon the subject, and to report to the church." April 17th this committee reported in such manner, that a committee of two was appointed " to bring forward a complaint against Brother Williams." Mr. Williams was served with a copy of the same. April 28th the complaint was read before the church, to which Mr. Williams pleaded not guilty. Three witnesses were brought forward; two of them " positively asserted " that Brother Williams said " By God." The third " was not so confident, but rather thought he did." In behalf of Mr. Williams, one witness testified he heard only the word " By." A second said he " positively knew " it was " By George." The church voted the complaint sustained, and Brother Williams was suspended till such time as he should make satisfaction. Mr. Williams was not content with this, and a mutual council was called. This council stated as its opinion " that they did not consider the charge against him supported in manner and form as alleged in the complaint." But the council proceeded to admonish Brother Williams " to take special heed to his ways in the future that he offend not with his tongue." The council also regretted that the church had not pressed the steps with Brother Williams pointed out in the eighteenth chapter of Matthew, and advised that the church consider Mr. Williams' submission to their verdict ground for his restoration. Some desired it be deferred for a season, but at length concluded to restore Mr. Williams.

Nearly four weeks later the church met and reconsidered its vote in accepting and approving the result of the council, and voted to offer him the choice of another mutual council. Mr. Williams, grieved and uneasy in his situation, desired that the grievance might be laid before the association for their advice. This the church refused to do, but voted they would unite with him in the choice of a mutual council if he desired it. This he declined.

A committee consisting of John Bliss, Samuel Sexton, and Calvin Stebbins was chosen to confer with Brother Williams

" to see if some method could not be adopted to heal the unhappy breach." This committee could effect nothing. At
this time Deacon Hitchcock desired a dismission from the
office of deacon, because " he was advanced in life and also on
account of some present circumstances." By " present circumstances " he meant the report Colonel Bliss made to an
ecclesiastical council of the proceedings of a committee on the
case of Mr. Williams, of which he was one. He supposed
them to be misrepresented. No vote by the church; they adjourned because it was late. On Friday, the 24th, the church
met. Deacon Hitchcock was asked whether he still persisted
in his request to be dismissed from serving as deacon. He
answered, " Yes." The church voted not to dismiss him for
the reasons assigned. The deacon said he must decline
serving. Nothing further was observed against the conduct
of Brother Bliss, either by Deacon Hitchcock or the members
of his committee; " but from what he then observed to them
and from the offers he made the matter seemed to be wholly
dropt." More than a year after this Deacon Hitchcock desired a certificate of regular standing and dismission from this
church " to the church in the north parish or any other regular
church where he might occasionally desire communion."
* Note "H."

Dr. Stebbins asks, " Where is Brother Williams? " He
adds, " Not a ray of light is thrown upon his destiny; he is left
suspended between the church and the world in perilous
proximity to the latter." I find evidence to the contrary. It
is my belief he was restored to church membership, for against
his name is written in Mr. Warren's handwriting, in the old
book kept by him, now extant, " Removed," which means, according to a note inserted in the new records copied from the
old, " Removed by letter to another church." A careful
reading of the record of these proceedings, as it was kept by
Mr. Warren, convinces me that the church was obliged to
take some action by the fact of Mr. Williams' " voluntary confession." In its proceedings it sought simply the truth. The
weight of evidence was that he had been profane, which
certainly was ground for suspension. From the fact that
the advisability of making him a member of the church
was questioned, and also that the church found ground
to reconsider its vote to reinstate him, it would seem that all

was not straight about him. According to Congregational usage, the church was right in refusing the appeal to an association and desiring a mutual council. It was not that the church wanted " more time " to consider the matter of adopting the advice of the council, but that some thought his reinstating ought to be deferred, and that the church as a whole later became of this opinion. It was, moreover, more than a year after this trouble that Deacon Hitchcock asked for a letter of dismission.

Mr. Warren's account of the trouble does not reveal any spirit of malice, but simply the desire on the part of the church to keep herself pure. In a word, if John Bliss misrepresented Deacon Hitchcock, according to Mr. Warren's account he made such offers that the whole matter was dropped, and Deacon Hitchcock remained a year and more in the church. Mr. Williams was restored, and lived so well that he was granted, at some later date, a letter of dismission as one in good standing to another church. * Note "I."

I have dwelt on this case so long to correct any wrong impressions, but mainly because I believe it was in part this purifying process that made possible the great revival which came later in Mr. Warren's ministry.

During the time of this controversy the parish raised in 1793 £246 15s. to finish the meeting-house and see it glassed. Things now went on smoothly until in 1807, at a meeting of the church on June 7th, " conversation was had upon some matters of grievance " which John Bliss had against Elizur Tillotson, Jr.

This Colonel John Bliss was one of the most prominent citizens of the place. He had represented the town in the Legislature as early as 1773, and was a member of the three provincial congresses. He was also a member of the first Senate under the Constitution of 1780, and for many years afterwards. He had commanded a regiment in the Revolution, and was the only field officer in the war from the town. He was a judge of the Court of General Sessions, or Common Pleas, for the County of Hampden, for many years.

Elizur Tillotson, Jr., was keeper of one of the taverns in the village. From time to time he had applied to the courts where Mr. Bliss was one of the judges, for a license — which had been granted. When in 1807 he applied as before, his

application was met by a remonstrance from some of the leading men of the parish, disapproving of his request and stating
that his place was not a proper one for a tavern, nor was his
condition such as would enable him to keep a house of any
benefit to the public.   This was signed by John Bliss, Robert
Sessions, Comfort Chaffee, Jr., William and Eneas Clark,
Jonathan and Levi Flynt, Joseph Morris, Edward Morris,
David Burt, Noah Sexton, and nine others. *   Mr. Tillotson
failed to get his license.   This, of course, angered him against
those who had signed the petition, and chiefly against Judge
Bliss.   Tillotson's course was such as to cause Mr. Bliss to
bring the matter before the church in the following letter:

"Reverend and Beloved: From a sense of duty and
anxious for the interests of religion in this place I am con-
strained to exhibit a complaint against our brother Elizur Tillotson Jun. which comprises two or three articles of grievance.
viz.   In that he said last fall when he returned from North-
ampton that I lied and he could prove it.   And also that if I
and General Shepard and one more had been dead or in our
graves where we ought to have been years ago he should have
obtained his license.   And further, that upon hearing of the
death of Captain Stebbins, he observed that the Lord had
begun a good work, and that if he would proceed and carry off
Col. Bliss, Comfort Chaffee and John Goodwell we should
have good times; all of which I think are contrary to a christian
profession, and I desire the church to take them under consideration and to proceed with Brother Tillotson as the gospel
directs."

The result of it all was that Mr. Tillotson was censured,
then suspended, and at last restored.   Mr. Bliss confessed to
some "unhappy expressions" in his complaint, and asked forgiveness of any whose feelings he had hurt.   By the narrating
of these things, unpleasant though they be, it is made
manifest that the church kept a strict watch over its members,
seeking to hold them to a gospel standard of confession for
wrong and effort for future right doing.   In this way I conceive that with a faithful man and biblical preacher in the
pulpit, the soil was prepared and the seed sown which resulted
in a magnificent harvest in 1822.

---

* The nine others were: Wm Clark, Asa Isham, Samuel Sexton, Walter Shaw, Jared
Case, Wm. Wood, Lemuel Jones, Charles Sessions, and Nathaniel B. Chaffee.—J. F. M.

In the natural world the husbandman looketh for a harvest only when he has made ready for it. There is many a farm in our own town richly productive to-day which years ago would not have borne half it now does; there were rocks and snags to be gotten out, wet places to be drained, which called for toil from the early morning to the late evening. Even so is it in the spiritual kingdom; so was it in the days of Warren. For thirty years he labored faithfully, and the result of his toil began to show when, in about 1820, a revival spirit took possession of the people. Meetings were held, and some ten united with the church and became working Christians. In a letter written in February, 1822, from Andover by Horace Sessions to his brother Sumner, it appears that Horace had been contracting for a number of volumes of the *Missionary Herald* for subscribers in Wilbraham. He expresses surprise at the large number of subscriptions procured. "I cannot conceive," he says, "how you accomplished it." Here is index of an interest in spiritual things; an interest deep enough to touch people's pockets.

But another voice was destined to rouse the people's hearts more intensely, and with our good parson, then sixty-four years of age, to reap for the Lord a harvest, the like of which this church never knew before, nor has known since.

In the early part of May, 1822, the Rev. Asahel Nettleton retired from New Haven to Somers for the purpose of recovering his health, which was much impaired by sickness. A few weeks after he arrived, a report reached the people that there was some religious excitement at Somers, and that a Mr. Nettleton was there attending one or two evening meetings during the week. Indeed, it was shortly announced that there were several persons anxious for their souls. Awakened by principles of curiosity, or through the influence of other motives, some of the young people in the place concluded to go down and test the verity of these reports. The evening fixed upon was Friday, June 21st, and a number at an early hour repaired to the house of worship in Somers. To their astonishment they found a crowded audience and awful solemnity pervading. The subject of humble submission to Christ was effectually enforced. To some of these visitors it proved to be a word in season. One young person was in such anxiety as to be unable to return, and therefore tarried in one of the families of the neighborhood.   The next day she expressed a hope of having passed from death to life.

This, with other circumstances, awakened with Mr. Nettleton an interest in the people of South Wilbraham.   Express invitations were at this time, as well as previously, forwarded by the minister and individuals urging Mr. Nettleton to visit South Wilbraham.   On Tuesday afternoon, June 25th, Mr. Nettleton, for the first time, consented to have an appointment made for him in the hall at sunset.   This appointment, though of a few hours' previous notice, like an electric shock reached every extremity of the society.   At the set time the room was literally crowded, and multitudes were yet assembling. Mr. Nettleton took his station, from which in the hall little else was to be seen than a dense surface of expressive countenances, and at the same time from the windows might be seen trees and roofs of adjacent buildings occupied by anxious hearers.   The preacher's subject was, " The ground of alarm to awakened sinners."

Many were roused to anxiety.   These scenes were new and interesting to the people.   There had never been a general revival in the place from its first settlement till this time, and the language of every heart seemed to be " what do these things mean."   It would be an injustice to the opposers of religion not to mention that they acted their part well.   Slanderous reports and insinuations of every kind were current against Mr. Nettleton.   Much opposition was offered by the Universalists.   At one time a meeting was appointed in the Bull Hill schoolhouse.   One Reuben Hendricks stood at the door with a club determined to break up the meeting.   This he succeeded in doing; but Captain Comfort Chaffee opened his house to the people and Mr. Nettleton preached there from the parable of the Pharisee and the Publican.   Still the opposition continued.   " I had rather sickness would visit my family than Nettleton," said one.   Said another, " If he visits this place we shall have a famine."   Others said, "Now this excitement shall not be, we will put a stop to it; it is really becoming a serious evil; when business gets to this pass, it is time that we interfere."   Had the smallest living atom proposed to create a world it would not have appeared more ridiculous than did these anti-religious reasoners stopping a revival in a dignified manner.   As in a moment they found their refuge of lies swept away by the powerful influence of God's Spirit.

But Satan now mustered all his forces; not a drunkard, profane person, or Sabbath-breaker in the place who was not candid in saying he was very much alarmed at this growing evil, a revival; and that he thought it intolerable to have such an ado about religion, and he thought it his duty to discountenance it. During this opposition, Mr. Nettleton, so far as his health would permit, was rallying the consciences of one and another as he had opportunity to subjects of greater moment than of opposition to religion. On June 27th a letter was received from President Nott, containing an extract from the minutes of the Albany Presbytery, in which were expressed the sentiments of approbation which this body cherished toward the Rev. Mr. Nettleton; and in which the Presbytery requested him " to furnish them with a detailed memorial of the causes helping the increase and hastening the decline of revivals of religion."

The doctor then added: " If it were necessary for me to add my testimony to that of the Presbytery, I should say, no man ever left us sustaining a more unblemished character or held in more affectionate remembrance than Mr. Nettleton. His labors of love here will long be remembered by our churches."

A friend of Mr. Nettleton's showed this letter to the more respectable opposers. This, with other circumstances, seemed to carry conviction to every mind of the impotency of opposition. On the evening of this 27th of June Mr. Nettleton met his second appointment in the church, which was full and solemn. There no longer remained a, doubt of the presence of God by the special influence of his Spirit among the people. Many were anxiously inquiring, " Men and brethren what shall we do? "

From this time forward the work advanced rapidly. Let us enter the church and listen to one of the sermons. The text is of Dives and Lazarus. Mr. Nettleton begins by saying it is not a parable; the Scripture says there *was* a .rich man. He goes on to say the moment a man dies he is in happiness or misery. Next, the request of the rich man indicates that this misery is very tormenting. The answer, that between God and Dives there is a fixed gulf, indicates that this torment is unalleviated.

Dr. Todd, in the life of his father, speaks of having been much impressed with this sermon which he heard at New Haven. One of its hearers in this church describes it as an awful sermon under which the audience fairly quailed. By such preaching the young were deeply affected. At the close of one meeting a young woman was overwhelmed with a sense of her guilt. As she dwelt some distance from the village she was asked by one of her companions living near to spend the night with her. At midnight Mr. Nettleton was sent for to come to this house. It was filled with people. He found the young woman sustained in the arms of her friends, piteously crying out, " Lord Jesus, have mercy on my soul." The next day, while in a company of young people with whom Mr. Nettleton was talking, she, with one or two others, expressed joy and peace in believing.

On Thursday, July 11th, Mr. Nettleton met sixty or eighty in an anxious meeting — an awful scene of distress. From this they went to the church, where he spoke on the danger of grieving the Spirit of God. It was indeed a heart-searching subject. The sobs and sighs of anxious sinners were to be heard from all parts of the house. At its close a large number rushed towards Mr. Nettleton as if expecting assistance from him. Many cried out aloud and the house was filled with groans of distress. The multitude clambered upon the rear seats, beholding with astonishment these effects of the Holy Spirit of God opening the eyes of the blind and loosing the tongues of the dumb. Mr. Nettleton addressed them for about five minutes and asked them to retire as quietly as possible. Some were so overwhelmed that it became necessary to urge and even assist them home. By Monday, the 29th of July, thirty had been converted. At an anxious meeting on the evening of this day, in the village hall, there were at least a hundred and fifty present. At the close of the meeting, which was peculiarly interesting, there was witnessed the most intense scene of distress known thus far during the revival; there was evidenced generally a more deep conviction of sin than at any previous meeting. As the people passed on to the green retiring from the hall, there was a burst of feeling among the more anxious, which one may imagine was a faint expression of the agonies of the damned on receiving their final doom.

Flying to each other's arms, in piercing cries they exclaimed, " I am sinking to hell, I am sinking to hell." They were immediately led by their friends to the house of Mr. Warren, just across the street, where for a time were responded from one room to another cries which were calculated to melt the hardest heart. Never did the justice and mercy of God united in a work of grace appear to move in greater majesty than on this occasion. The voice of opposition for a time was hushed to silence, and many by what they witnessed were converted. On the next day a number who were in such distress on the preceding evening expressed a hope of having submitted, and the number of anxious sinners was very much increased.

From this time on the work steadily advanced until nearly one hundred had expressed a faith in Christ, and at the communion in October sixty-two were received into the church, among whom was our present senior deacon, William V. Sessions.

Surely they who labor faithfully God does not overlook; in His own time he sends the blessing. I love to linger on this period; it is to me surrounded with a holy light; it is the picture of a man living to see God's magnificent blessing on his lifelong work.

But I must hasten to give you a summary of Mr. Warren's pastorate, and, with some estimate of this your first pastor, pass on to the next.

His pastorate was forty years long. During it he admitted to the church 262, an average of about six a year. He baptized 478, married 226 couples, and educated for college a dozen young men.

In November, 1828, the church assembled to lay away Lydia, the wife of Mr. Warren, at the age of 73. She was the daughter of Colonel Bliss, and for thirty-nine years had been a vigorous-minded, courageous, and faithful wife.

Not long after this Mr. Warren was himself taken sick with some affection of the lungs. It was winter, he was an old man, and he could not get well. During this sickness his thoughts turned especially to spiritual things, and he made an effort to give utterance to the fullness of his feelings. When nature was nearly exhausted he bade good-bye to his family, and peacefully fell asleep. . . . Three months after the

funeral of Lydia Warren the church assembled again, this
time to bury their spiritual father. Mr. Strong of Somers
preached the funeral sermon; then they went to the hillside
yonder and laid him away. Side by side they buried them,
man and wife; the weeping willow on the headstone marks
the people's grief, and words beneath, " I am the resurrection
and the life; he that believeth on me, tho' he were dead, yet
shall he live," tell their happy state.

Of Mr. Warren it becomes us to say that he possessed the
characteristic indispensable in a minister — a self-distrust in
his own powers, not great enough to allow him to do less than
his best, but sufficient to make him constantly depend on God
for his guidance and blessing. This made him peculiarly a
man of prayer. It is the witness of those who knew him as a
brother minister that they were deeply moved by this characteristic of the man; and his oldest living listener, in all that she
had forgotten of his ministry, yet remembered especially the
words of his public prayers.

With these traits so prominent, it is easy to see how he became remarkable for his piety. None ever doubted that.
I do not believe you could find a man or woman who themselves ever questioned, or heard questioned, the goodness of
Parson Warren. This is to me peculiarly significant, and will
find its place of comment further on. . . . Mr. Warren possessed a good knowledge of Scripture facts. His education
had been as complete as the times afforded, and there is every
indication that he stood well intellectually with his ministerial
associates.

One thing more; he was a man of large sympathy. If a
beggar came to his door at meal time, he would rise and serve
the beggar before he himself ate. You will know then by his
act to a stranger what he was to the people he loved.

Were not the conditions to success united in this man, and
is it any wonder that the revival which so moved this vicinity
in the first quarter of the century visited the church to which
he ministered?

> "He is gone who seemed so good.
> Gone ; but nothing can bereave him
> Of the force he made his own
> Being here ; and we believe him
> Something far advanced in state,
> And that he wears a truer crown
> Than any wreath that man can weave him."

Lucius W. Clark, the second pastor of the church, was installed December 9, 1829, about nine months after the death of Mr. Warren. He was a native of Mansfield, Conn., graduated at Brown University in 1825, and studied theology with Dr. Ide of Medway in this State. When he came to the church here he was twenty-eight years old. There was, therefore, a great contrast between Mr. Warren and Mr. Clark. The former was at his death seventy-three years of age; he had been in the parish long enough to know all its members; he was a man mild by nature, so that it was not easy for a young man with almost no experience to follow the first pastor — by nature, knowledge, and experience so fitted to lead the church. It has been recorded of Mr. Clark that he little understood the temper of the people, and therefore brought in dissensions which resulted in his going away. It is the desire of your historian, while telling the exact truth, to throw the mantle of charity over those upon whom censure may have fallen.

So far as my own researches have gone I find in Mr. Clark purity of motive in his work, but a lack of wisdom in method, which is, perhaps, to be partly accounted for by his youth. In proof of this let me cite a case which occurred in 1831. A certain brother had for some time absented himself from communion. The records imply that he was suspended. Later on he complained that no written accusation had been lodged against him, and so I suppose asked to be restored, for I find record to the effect that no written complaint being presented the church voted to forgive Brother ———— and restore him to the fellowship of the church. · After this record Mr. Clark put several exclamation marks, and then added: " A man who for more than a year has trampled upon the institutions of Christ's house, yet is suffered to pass with impunity even while manifesting hostility to the church, shall not God visit such a church with the rod." To Mr. Clark the case was a clear one. He saw it in but one light; expressed his opinion by strong words and exclamation marks. His motive was right; he desired the purity of the church. His method wrong; if he believed the brother at fault he should have left his opinion unwritten, and made its intensity the motive to his effort to get hold of the brother and win him, by leading him back.

I think it safe to say he failed of the best success because he

5

tried to drive, rather than lead, his people.   The preaching of Mr. Clark was of that unyielding sort which in some cases conciliated not so much as it antagonized.

Let us lay, as I have already suggested, this lack of wisdom in method, while we admit the purity of motive, to the pastor's youth and inexperience, and turn to the good that was done under his pastorate.

When Mr. Clark came to the church it numbered 107, 33 males and 74 female members.   Of the original members there still remained Zadoc Stebbins, Joseph Bumstead, and Lucy Morris.   During his pastorate of three years 22 were admitted to the church, 21 of them by profession of faith, three of whom are still with us; 16 were baptized, 11 children and 5 adults.   An effort was also made to increase the spiritual interests of the church by excluding from the communion those who were unfitted for it, and by appointing a committee to visit all the members and talk with them separately on matters of religion.

During this ministry, on the 23d of February, 1832, the "Ladies' Benevolent Society" was formed, the object of which was "to raise funds by means of manual labor for the purpose of promoting some benevolent object."   Mrs. Clark, Mrs. Flynt, and Mrs. Betsy Warren were the first directors.

Mr. Clark left here in December, 1832.   For some time he preached as stated supply in the Fifth Church of Plymouth. He died at Middlebury in 1854 at the age of fifty-three.

From here on, your historian finds his task, in many places, an exceedingly unsatisfactory one.   The church records are silent from October 5, 1833, to December 31, 1838, except in so far as to record the names of those admitted to the church and those baptized.   Even after the coming of Mr. Hazen, with the exception of one case of discipline, nothing is recorded except as before the names of the baptized and admitted from 1839 to December, 1846 — in all a period of thirteen years. Here and there a paper is to be found in the possession of some individual; these, as they offer clues, with what lives in the memory of the people, must form the substance of our story for many years.

Between the dismission of Mr. Clark in 1832 and the ordination of Mr. Hazen in 1839, the church was supplied by Mr. Wright, Mr. Brockaway, and others.   Mr. Wright was called "a saintly man"; Mr. Brockaway "a superior preacher." One man came for some time whom the people thought of settling, but found him unfit for the trust. After his departure the records of the church's doings were found scattered on the floor. During this period 19 were admitted to the church, 8 by profession, 11 by letter; 18 were baptized, 17 children, 1 adult.

On the 31st of December, 1838, the church voted unanimously to call as its pastor James A. Hazen. He accepted the call and was ordained January 30, 1839. Mr. Hazen came from West Springfield. He was graduated at Yale College in 1834, and later at the New Haven Theological Seminary.

This was one of the very prosperous and happy pastorates of the church. In it 15 were admitted and 24 were baptized. The great event, however, was the remodeling of the church.

As the building stood on the green it was a source of annoyance, because it marred very greatly the looks of the street. In 1817, and again in 1822 and 1824, attempts were made to remove it, but without success. Now it was old-fashioned; ideas of church architecture had changed. In 1838, on the 13th of February, a meeting of the citizens of the South Parish was held " to take into consideration the propriety of moving and repairing the meeting-house belonging to said parish." John B. Morris was moderator of the meeting, and R. S. Chapin clerk. A committee of seven was chosen to examine and report the probable expense of moving and repairing, also the expense of a site. These seven were Samuel Beebe, Beriah Smith, William V. Sessions, Aaron Warren, Stephen S. West, Ralph S. Chapin, and Charles Sessions. This committee reported on Tuesday, February 20th, as follows: " The expense of moving the house $50. Expense of site on Captain Session's corner, including his garden amounting to sixty rods of ground to be cleared of buildings, $300. Should the parish agree to purchase the above, Captain Sessions pledges himself to pay $5 for every $100 that shall be raised for moving and repairing. Expense of basement not to exceed $200, a total of $550."

On the first of March following a committee of five was chosen to draft and circulate a subscription paper to obtain money for these purposes. On the 15th inst. a committee of five, consisting of Beriah Smith, Sumner Sessions, William V.

Sessions, Samuel Stebbins, and Aaron Warren, was appointed to superintend the moving, and begin as soon as practicable. A subscription paper was started, dated March 2, 1838, under four heads: First, for new site and moving; second, basement story; third, steeple; fourth, slips, etc.

Some gave for one and would not give for others; a few gave for all four purposes. The building was moved in the summer of 1838, but sufficient money to repair the church as desired was not raised, and in January, 1840, another paper was circulated. It read as follows:

" A celebrated and pious writer once observed that it did not become a community of Christians to decorate their dwelling houses and neglect the house of public worship. Although it is delightful to render to our Maker the homage of a grateful, penitent, and obedient heart in any situation, still no place can be made too convenient or delightful for this purpose. Being fully aware that the Congregational meeting-house in the south parish of Wilbraham is far from being elegant, comfortable, or convenient, and desiring at least in some manner to make it so, the undersigned hereby agree to pay the several sums annexed to our names to Samuel Beebe, Noah Langdon, William V. Sessions, Ralph S. Chapin, and Marcius Cady for the purpose of repairing said house, lessening the room in height to the distance of 15 or 16 feet in the clear or length of posts by erecting another floor at such distance above the present one as to leave the aforesaid distance in the height of the room and fit it up in a convenient, workmanlike manner conformably to the principles of modern style; subscriptions to be paid when the work is completed."

Sums appear to the amount of $1,023. Other subscriptions were added to these, and the work was carried on. The gallery, pews, and floor were taken out; a new raised floor was laid; rooms were built below; ten feet were added for a belfry; a bell was bought in Boston, and in December, 1840, the building as repaired was dedicated, the sermon being preached by the pastor.

During the pastorate of Mr. Hazen great efforts were made to popularize in the place the millerite views of the second coming of Christ and the end of the world in 1843. Papers and books were circulated, especially " The Midnight Cry "; and many lectures delivered. To Mr. Hazen the whole thing was "a baseless speculation and calculated to exert a most pernicious influence on the interests of true religion." He felt it his duty to expose its fallacy and to exhibit what he considered the truth. He therefore delivered in 1842 some discourses aimed at the false doctrine. I write of this with the object not only of giving you the point of history, but also because hereby I shall be able to show you the man. The task was a most unpleasant and painful one, undertaken only from an imperious sense of duty to his fellow men and of accountability to God. At the close of one of the sermons which was published, he says: "Holding as I do the most responsible of public stations, I should prove recreant to the vows of my office if, through fear of giving offence or of subjecting myself to misrepresentation, I should sit supinely by and see what I regard as a most baleful delusion sweeping through the community. May God give me grace never to fear to speak the whole truth when duty demands it, even though I shall thereby drive from me my nearest friends." Measured by the standard of the prophecy of Ezekiel, shall we not give our commendation to the course of Mr. Hazen as to one who loved God and His truth, loved his fellow better than his own popularity, and yet possessed such method in his work, speaking logically, historically, and scripturally, and with such spirit, that the cause of truth was benefited and he himself unhurt.

In 1847 Mr. Hazen asked for his dismission from the pastorate of the church because of ill health. The church was reluctant to have him go; they advised him to take a journey and to use all other means to better his physical condition. But Mr. Hazen still thought it best that he should be released, and was accordingly dismissed June 22, 1847.

He afterwards settled in South Williamstown, and at Lisbon, Conn., where he died October 29, 1862, at the age of forty-nine. His body was at his request brought here for burial, and was placed beside that of the wife and child whom twenty years before he had laid to rest.

In less than six months after the dismission of Mr. Hazen the church voted unanimously to invite the Rev. Hubbard Beebe to become its pastor. He accepted the invitation, and was installed on the 19th of April, 1848.

Mr. Beebe, who was a native of Richmond, Mass., came to South Wilbraham with the double experience of preacher and schoolteacher. He graduated at Williams College in 1833, and later at Andover. He was ordained at Long-meadow, October 18, 1837, where he labored five and a half years. From there he went to Westfield and became a teacher in the academy. From Westfield he came to this church. We shall find that his work here was a two-fold one in its results; first, church-wise, and second, in giving impulse to secular education.

Following a particularly good man, himself gifted and popular as a preacher, Mr. Beebe reaped a good harvest in the four years of his life here, 26 being added to the church, 18 by profession. In September of 1848 the church voted to adopt in place of its first covenant and confession of faith those of the First Church in Springfield.

The form of union under which the church was organized was a covenant and confession combined. With the exception of one instance it did not distinctly say " we believe," but implied that " believe " when it said " We give up ourselves to the Lord Jehovah, the one only living and true God, subsisting in three persons, Father, Son, and Holy Ghost, equal in power and glory." This way of stating their belief does not seem always to have given satisfaction; for I find, on the authority of tradition, that a confession of faith in manuscript form was long used asking for the assent of the one presenting himself for membership to a definite " You believe."

The first confession spoke of God in the trinity, as did also the second; the first spoke of baptism and the Lord's supper — on these the second was silent; the first mentioned Christ's ascension and the consequent giving of pastors and teachers; the second made no particular mention of these. On the other hand the second affirmed man's sin and misery caused by disobedience; pointed to Christ as the one " bearing the curse and answering the law " for man; affirmed its belief in a justification by faith; in the Scriptures of the Old and New Testaments as God's word; in a second coming of Christ, and a consequent everlasting punishment for the wicked and happiness for Christians. The first had a covenant with a confession implied; the second a confession with a distinct covenant added. But the confession lacked some of the essential features of the church's belief, like the Sacraments; and the covenant, while it asked for the promise of the one joining the church, offered no promise in return from those already members.

Seeking for reasons for the change to the confession and covenant of the Springfield church, from a study of the first and second confessions and covenants, these have appeared to me, in want of any direct testimony, to be sufficient.

The " Articles of Faith," so called, adopted in 1848, is the one now in use in the church. It is very full and perfectly orthodox; admits of no probation after death, but makes the day of judgment the time when " the state of all will be unalterably fixed." One thing especially strong about it is that it fortifies its statements with a great many Scriptural references, as many as seventy-five being given in one instance. The covenant embraces a promise on the part of the one joining the church, and also those who receive him, which the old did not.

This work will indicate Mr. Beebe as a man progressive according to that idea of progress which while it loses nothing of the past which has been good, the rather seeks to hold that good by adding more to it; a principle not always observed in the matter of church creeds.

The enterprise of the man also appears in the stimulus which he gave to secular education in the town. There were a good many young people here in his day, and by working at them, and through them, he roused the parents to an active sense of the young people's needs in educational privileges. It followed that an association was formed by several gentlemen of the town, with the object, as they stated in their first prospectus, " of establishing upon a permanent basis a select school in this village to secure a more thorough and extensive course of instruction for our youth."

The committee for the association announced to the public that in the village of South Wilbraham, beautiful in its natural scenery and healthy in its physical and moral atmospheres, a select school had been thus established. A neat and convenient building had been erected, having a large schoolroom and two recitation-rooms on the first floor, and a fine hall on the second; that the building was furnished with maps, charts, and philosophical apparatus; that the course of instruction under the direction of Mr. George Brooks, the principal, would be such as to secure to the pupil a thorough and practical training. The common branches taught would be from Colburn's First Lessons, Thompson's Arithmetic, Goldthwait's Grammar, Smith's Geography, and Wilson's United States History.

The higher branches would embrace Algebra, Euclid, Natural Philosophy, Chemistry, Physiology, Philosophy of Natural History, Botany, Intellectual Philosophy, Ancient Geography, General History, and the Latin Language. The committee also gave parents the assurance that careful attention would be paid to the formation of correct tastes and habits in study, and to the general deportment of pupils; that a healthy state of moral and religious feeling would be regarded of the utmost importance, and that the Bible would be the text book in the daily religious exercises and instructions of the school. The total expenses of each pupil for the year were not to exceed $88.50.

Afterwards the school passed under the direction of Mr. Wood, as its principal; and Trigonometry, Astronomy, Political Economy, Bookkeeping, Rhetoric, Psychology, Logic, with the Greek, French, and German languages, and a course in vocal music were added to the curriculum.

Of the effects of the school it must suffice us here to say that an educational impetus was given to the town which is being felt to-day.

Mr. Beebe was dismissed from the church on the 24th of March, 1852. He afterwards labored with the churches at Sturbridge and West Haven, Conn., and then became in turn secretary of the American Sabbath-school Union, agent of the American Bible Society, and associate secretary of the American Seaman's Friend Society. He died of heart disease on the 21st of June last at Bethlehem, N. H., at the age of seventy-six, and against his name history will surely write — a faithful, persistent, and progressive worker in the kingdom of the Master.

For the next year and more after the dismission of Mr. Beebe, the pulpit was supplied by different men; some were called but declined to accept. Although the church had no pastor, a good deal of religious interest prevailed. Meetings were held at the house of Deacon Sumner Sessions, and in April, 1853, twenty-four were admitted to the church on profession of faith.

One day Deacon Sessions was riding along the street when he met a man who proved to be Rev. Mr. Galpin of West Stafford.

The conversation turned to church matters, when the deacon said that it was very hard to find supplies for the pulpit, and added that they had no one for the next Sabbath. The minister answered that he knew of a man, a graduate of the last class at Andover, who was that week coming to his house, and could preach here the next Sunday.

He came and preached, seemed to be the man for the hour, and so it was decided to call him. Thus the church obtained its fifth pastor, Rev. E. S. Skinner, who was ordained May 19, 1853.

Mr. Skinner was a native of Plattsburg, N. Y., graduated at Oberlin College in 1849, and then at Andover Seminary. He was the active pastor of the church for one year only, so that the story of his work is soon told.

The religious interest prevalent at the time of his coming continued, and four were received to the church at the next communion on profession.

The church now for the first time chose a standing committee of three to act in connecton with the pastor and deacons. She also showed her life by appointing committees to print the articles of faith adopted under Mr. Beebe and to revise the records of the church; a sort of spiritual taking account of stock and bringing before the members her condition, and putting in their hands her new creed as the motive and measure of future activity.

During his college and seminary course, by reason of overwork, Mr. Skinner contracted a bronchial trouble, which, during his first year here, assumed an inflammatory form. This so unfitted him for his work that he was obliged to give up preaching. The trouble increasing, at the end of a year he asked to be dismissed, and was released from this charge April 11, 1855.

The same council which dismissed him installed his successor, the Rev. James C. Houghton. He was born at Lyndon, Vt., May 13, 1810. He spent three years at Amherst College, and graduated at Dartmouth in 1837, and at the Theological Institute of Connecticut in 1840. He was ordained as an evangelist at Storrsville in Petersham, of this

6

state, December 22, 1840, where he supplied till April, 1843. From 1843 to 1845 he was acting pastor at East Hartland, Conn., and Granby, Conn., from 1845 to 1847. From September 15, 1847, to February, 1851, he was settled at Middle Haddam, and for the two years and a half following at Nepaug in New Hartford. The next year he came to South Wilbraham, remaining till October 1, 1856, about seventeen months.

The day of the installation there was a driving snow storm, which also is true of the days of Mr. Hazen's and Mr. Beebe's installations, with rain instead of snow at Mr. Skinner's.

The sermon of the installation day was preached by Mr. Colton of Monson from Paul's words written to Timothy in the Second Epistle, the first five verses of the fourth chapter.

Standing as I do thirty years after the time of Mr. Houghton, and, therefore, able to judge impartially, seeking as you have made it incumbent on me to give a true picture of the past, I cannot but state it as my opinion that Mr. Houghton left the pastorate of the church because he obeyed implicitly the words of the ordination text.

He came from a seminary ever characterized by its faithful adherence to the Bible in its every part. He was a man of strong convictions, based on a careful study of the Word. The creed of the church, which he came to uphold, in its second article says: " We believe that the Scriptures are profitable for doctrine, for correction, for reproof, for instruction in righteousness." It fortifies its position by the words of Timothy beginning " Every Scripture is profitable for teaching." The creed of the church, in its ninth article, commits itself to the doctrine of election, and cites in its support Paul's words written in Romans viii, 30.

The preaching of this doctrine was the small end of the wedge, which, entering, more and more finally severed the pastoral relationship of Mr. Houghton from the church.

It is but fair to say that the church's creed has sixteen articles, so that, other things being equal, one article might not claim more than one-sixteenth of the Sundays' sermons. Yet if the preacher saw any lack of adherence to the church's stated belief, his fidelity to the Master, to his own convictions, and to the church would become the motive to his dwelling upon a particular subject.

The council, which on September 9th advised the dismission embodied in its result, put in writing by men so discreet as Mr. Vaille and Mr. Harding, these words: "We wish it understood that we do not come to this result (the dissolving of the pastoral relation of Mr. Houghton and the church) from any want of confidence in him as a preacher of the doctrines of the cross and a faithful minister of Christ. And we cannot but embody in this result a word of caution to this church and people lest they allow too slight causes and misapprehensions to interrupt their Christian harmony; and also a word of exhortation that they maintain firmly and unwaveringly the doctrines of grace as held in their confession of faith."

Mr. Houghton accordingly went away. He worked afterwards for eight years at Chelsea, Vt., at Royalton, and in other fields for seven years more. He died of apoplexy at the house of his son in Montpelier on the 29th of April, 1880, and his name has passed into history with the words "An earnest preacher."

The wedge which separated Mr. Houghton and the church entered the church itself to the disturbing of its peace. The caution of the council was not, however, without its effect. The church rose to a sense of her need; a meeting was held, a paper prepared acknowledging the unadvisedness of words spoken and asking the church members to forgive the past in all, and henceforth to go forward unitedly as the followers of Christ with Christian charity and fellowship; and they were asked also to pledge themselves " renewedly to seek the peace and prosperity of the church." In answer to this paper nearly the whole church rose in token of their pledge, and from that day to this, so far as I am aware, the church has never objected to its ministers on the ground of too much doctrinal preaching.

For five years the church now had no settled pastor. The pulpit was filled by Mr. Doe, Mr. Underwood, and Mr. Kittredge. During this time the church received to her membership thirty-five, twenty-six of them being by profession.

Beginning with the next pastorate, the telling of our story must assume a somewhat different form. Five of the pastors of the seventy-one years, whose story we have now told, have finished their labors and entered into their rest. One was in the work only a year, but the three following are still in the ministry. The estimate of these men and their methods of work belongs not to me to write, but to the hand of a later day. That estimate is in part now yours, who listened to their preaching, received their ministrations in your times of sorrow, and walked with them the streets of daily life. In the years to come we shall find passing away men long and closely identified with the church's progress; two who for many years walked these aisles as your servants and your leaders; with whom, because of their peculiar ministrations to you, our thought must carry for a little in remembrance of their lives and their work.

On the 29th of September, 1861, the church met and voted a unanimous call to Rev. John Whitehill. Mr. Whitehill, a young man of Scotch descent, working in a mill at Chicopee, had awakened the interest of Mr. Oviatt. Influenced by him, Mr. Whitehill went to Amherst, where he graduated in 1858, and then to Andover. South Wilbraham was, therefore, his first settlement.

For six and a half years he worked with the church, adding to its membership thirty, seventeen of them on profession of faith.

In November of 1865 Mr. Whitehill met with the very severe loss of his wife, a constant companion in his walks, a truly helpful woman in his work. The next year he, in company with the church, met with a second heavy loss in the death of Deacon John B. Morris.

Mr. Morris was converted in the revival of 1822, and the next year was made a deacon in the church; when he died at the age of seventy-seven he had, therefore, been in active service for forty-three years. Through all this time he had been a prominent man in the town, and the church and social circle as well; he had filled many of the town offices, and had represented it in the Legislature.

In early life Mr. Morris' aspiration had been for a collegiate education. But it seemed to fall to him to remain on the farm; and the same sweetness of disposition which ever characterized the man led him to forego his own tastes in obedience to his grandfather's and his father's desire.

We may be sure that if he had become a professional man he would have attained a real success. For in apprehension he was quick and accurate; he had a good voice and a happy expression, but, more than all, a most remarkable memory. A man said to me: " I used to be afraid I might forget how old I was, but I came to be at perfect rest on the matter, for I knew I could go to Deacon Morris and he would remember the year and day I was born." And he could, for he could remember when every child in the village was born, and when every building was raised.

This mental acumen and accuracy showed itself in his Christian faith. His knowledge here was thorough, and his faith he talked and sung and lived. One who knew him well says of him: " He was one of those Christians whose views of truth are so clear, and whose faith is so strong, and whose love to God is so warm and fresh that they enjoy upon earth something of the serenity of heaven."

One day in May of the year 1866, Mr. Morris sung with an aged friend the hymn beginning " All hail the power of Jesus' name," and spoke of the rapture he expected to feel when he sang it in heaven. A few days after, when in the field, he appeared drowsy and inattentive; he was helped to the house and medical aid called, but his disease proved to be paralysis, and therefore incurable.

When on his death-bed his children took up the refrain of the song he had sung; his tongue was now silenced, but his heart still voiced the music. The days of the sickness were soon done, and the realization came of the last stanza of that " Coronation ":

> " Oh, that with yonder sacred throng
> We at his feet may fall !
> We'll join the everlasting song,
> And crown Him Lord of all."

That which sixty years before had been written of Mr. Morris' grandfather, John Bliss, we may say of him:

> " Reflection long shall hover o'er his urn
> And faithful friendship boast the power to mourn.
> Peace to his shade, while truth shall point the rest,
> Lamented most by those who knew him best "

In this pastorate the church building called for the attention of the people; it was out of repair, something needed to be done. Accordingly, in the warrant issued for the parish meeting of March 24, 1868, an article was placed — the eighth — as follows: "To see what measures the parish will adopt to repair the inside of their church." The parish voted to make "*thorough repairs*," and chose a committee of three "to investigate and report." A week later this committee reported, their work was accepted, and the committee was increased to six. A subscription paper was drawn up and circulated, and the work of repair was begun.

The years of Mr. Whitehill's pastorate here had been years of change in the ministry of the neighboring pulpits, Wilbraham, Somers, East Longmeadow, and Monson; north, south, east, and west of him men had gone, and Mr. Whitehill added to the list by resigning himself in April, 1868, leaving here the first of June.

The church had now the double task of repairing the building and finding a pastor. The latter was accomplished three months after the dismission of Mr. Whitehill, and the Rev. Edward B. Chamberlain was installed as the eighth pastor of the society.

Meantime the work on the church was progressing; the entrance from the porch in front to the vestry was closed; the gallery which ran across the south side and was entered by winding stairs running from the porch gave way to the one you now see; the walls were frescoed in panels; the large pulpit, reached by several steps, was replaced by the one behind which I now stand. The seats were the same in which you are sitting, but running straight across and arranged with two aisles. The square windows with outside blinds were replaced by these long ones with the blinds inside; the long sofa behind the pulpit gave place to chairs; a new green carpet was laid, and on the 3d of March, 1869, the bell called the people to enter by the one new door, not two, as of old, and re-dedicated their house of worship — completed at a cost of $3,000.

Five years Mr. Chamberlain worked with the church, receiving into its communion thirty on profession of their faith and eleven by letter, an average of eight each year.

He resigned his pastorate on the 22d of February, 1874, and, leaving this charge at the end of the quarter, accepted a call to Sharon, Vt., where he now resides.

After a year in which an effort was made to secure Mr. Eldridge as pastor, which would have been successful but for a previous obligation, the parish voted to hire the Rev. E. P. Root for one year.

Before the year had expired, on the 13th of April, 1876,

the church voted to Mr. Root a unanimous call to settle, and on a fair day in the peaceful June, the church met to ordain and install him in a pastorate destined to be the longest since that of Mr. Hazen, and, as the day itself, more than usually peaceful, and to be severed with many regrets.

Besides the quiet growth of the church indicated by its conversions, there are two events in this pastorate that call for our special attention; the one of gain, the other of deep loss; the first, the readorning of the church edifice; the second, the death of Deacon Sumner Sessions.

At the annual meeting of the parish, March 27, 1883, it was voted that the parish committee devise ways and means to fresco the church. Two weeks later, the committee were instructed to fresco the church and make all needful repairs. The Ladies' Society, by a committee, were also to help in the matter of selecting patterns for the frescoing. As an incentive to the work, a new bell had been generously given by Mr. Francis C. Sessions of Columbus, Ohio. The outside of the house was painted and a new walk laid in front of the church from funds intended originally for the purchase of a bell. Subscriptions were made in money, the Ladies' Society gave their aid, lumber and work were donated, and with new carpets, re-upholstering of furniture, re-covered doors, and, not least, the chandelier given by Mr. Lucius Beebe and his family, the church was given the form in which you see it to-day. (Cost, $750.43.)

How great is the difference between this neat, glassed, and well-heated building and the meeting-house of your fathers which stood on the green, with its boarded windows, its hard seats, with no fire even in the coldest weather! How many changes external and internal there have been!

And now it becomes me to speak of one whose life extended through all these changes but the last; one who loved the church very dearly and made his own life tell in her progress, Sumner Sessions.

He was born on the 29th of December, 1797, between Christmas and New Year's, a goodly gift to the church and the community. Baptized by Mr. Warren and brought under the influence of Christian home and church training, he became converted and united with the church in 1820.

Such was his nature that everything to him was positive.

When he said " I believe," he meant it through and through.
Others might not have strong convictions upon certain religious matters; he must. Others might swerve from their
convictions; he never. So that from the first he became a
strong-faithed Christian, and the power of his convictions
made him an earnest worker. In the revival of 1822 he was
ever active, and so great was the confidence of the church in
him that it chose him deacon with Mr. Morris on the 31st of
January, 1823, at the age of twenty-five years.

The picture which these young men make for us is not one
often met with in church annals, I think. Deacons of the
church, the one twenty-five years old, the other thirty-three,
differently constituted by nature, and yet always the warmest
friends; of the same school of religious belief, and thus
through life a double power for the maintenance of the
church's faith.

Mr. Sessions was called " a true Puritan of the Crom-
wellian stamp," which, if I understand the term, means no
compromise with heresy or with evil. Of a given measure,
the question he asked himself was, " Is it right?" If
answered negatively, it received his unqualified resistance; if
affirmatively, his zealous, outspoken support. With this
strength of conviction was united a real humility. He was
neither " boastful nor haughty."

The strength he showed " was the strength which comes
from reliance on God "; and that God-given power made itself
felt in the home, in the church, in the world.

On the 3d of May, 1879, after a deaconship of fifty-six
years, he was excused, at his own request, from active service.
In the fall of that year, though still erect in form, his health
began serious to fail. On Sunday, the 18th of January, 1880,
when his strength was fast going, he was assisted to the bed,
and as he lay down he said: " I lie down now to rise again at
the last great day."

The three score years and ten had lengthened into the
eighty and three, but though the Angel of Death had so long
stayed his coming, the church and the world, and they who
loved him best, would fain have held him back to the sphere of
life he so materially influenced for good.

Let us cherish his memory with the fullness with which we
appreciate his faith and work.

Five months after the resignation of Mr. Root, which took effect the 1st of January, 1884, the church gathered May 28th to ordain and install the third and last of its " Edwards."

In the year and more which has elapsed since then I have but to record your act of revising the church membership, which makes it possible to say that all the members are accounted for, either as residents, as preferring to retain their membership here, though living elsewhere, or as placed upon a retired list because no clue can be gained to their places of residence.

To record also your change of covenant, in which you have sought a warmer expression of love to those you receive, and added your engagement to hold and promote cordial fellowship with the members of sister churches of the common Head, " that the Lord may be one and his name one in his churches throughout all generations."

Here my story of your past closes. All too poorly I feel it has been told.

While prominent facts could be stated and figures given, it must needs be that the individual consecration of heart, the self-sacrifice and intense effort of life uniting to make possible those facts and results expressed in figures should remain unwritten by reason of their multitude and the limits of the hour.

As we turn the page of the past and begin a new century of church life there are some voices speaking out of the past which we shall do well to heed.

The first is of a changed relationship between the church and a part of its constituency. In 1785 the parish officer collected by law from every man in the parish for the support of one church; 1885 finds four churches and many people who are not connected with any. The right which the early settler demanded of worshiping *where* he chose, the villager has now extended into a *how* he chooses.

The century has taught that men cannot be whipped into the church by legal thongs, but must be drawn in by a law affecting the heart.

The church has, then, to determine her attitude towards all denominations and consider how to reach the hearts of the unbelieving. That which differentiates denominations, that which differentiates Christians and non-Christians, is primarily difference of belief. The work of the century to come is, I think, to bring all men nearer to an outward union by means of an inward unity. This unity will come according as men approach nearer to Christ in fullness of knowledge and fullness of faith.

To my thought, compromise of belief does not increase the unity of St. Paul's standard. Therefore the denominational attitude of the church should be based on a fidelity to her own convictions of faith, at the same time exercising the largest charity to those of a different belief; striving herself and urging others to strive for the *complete knowledge* which is of the one Christ; realizing, too, that all churches are one in a union against sin, and in the pointing unbelievers to the Saviour.

The power of the church, too, in its individual desire to touch the hearts of unbelieving men, begins in its definite belief and the consequent action. The preaching of Mr. Nettleton and the life of Mr. Warren emphasize this. The revivalist said, " The moment a man dies his eternal state is fixed." This is a very definite statement; it shows that he walked easily where many to-day find themselves compelled to feel their way step by step. This one statement is easily matched by others in sermons on many different subjects. They all reveal a man of profoundly definite convictions, and by such preaching he persuaded men to believe. It is the history of this church that those converted under his preaching have been strong, unwavering, useful Christians; and I am sure that the same is true elsewhere.

The life of Mr. Warren, so remarkably pure, was in keeping with such a definite belief. Mr. Nettleton preached to the converting of men, and he did it here, and that is the very thing laid before us: to live a blameless life ourselves and persuade men to be with us imitators of the Christ. The past has left us as a real legacy, goodly belief, and we have made it the expression of our faith, and by God's help we can make it more the regulator of our lives.

So far, then, our task is plain, and the instruments to success in our hands; let us be wise enough not to carelessly put them out.

And now to this, the past adds one voice more. It comes from the days of 1822, it speaks from those of 1856, when the church was brought to better thought and renewed consecration; it tells in our ears the words, " Seek the Presence and Power of the Holy Spirit."

The Spirit who was the divine instrument in first bringing the natural order out of chaos; who in man's powerful struggle with sin, taught man to hope in a Messiah through whom he should be victorious; the Spirit, the promise of whose coming was the consoling blessing of the departing Master to his troubled disciples; and whose actual coming with Pentecostal fire bore witness to the reinstating in glory of the crucified but risen Christ, and pierced men's hearts with deep conviction of sin.

This Spirit who in the ages of the church ever since has been the effective agent of God; who in this place moved the hearts of the children and the youth, and they of mature years, to an overwhelming sense of sin, and then led them to the Christ to find forgiveness.

This Spirit, if we want him, will be our helper in the years to come.

Brethren, as we close these pages, the door of the future opens. Say not,'it is an unknown land; for the Divine Light is shining into it; the Father's Hand is held ready to lead us; and when our work is done, with those the story of whose lives has now been told, we also shall find place in the " Church of the First-Born enrolled in Heaven," and shall add our voices to the mighty chorus saying, " Worthy is the lamb that hath been slain, to receive power and riches, and wisdom and might, and honor and glory and blessing."

Unto Him be the glory of our salvation; unto him be the dominion universal, forever and forever. Amen.

NOTES.

The petition for the division of the town was as follows:

To the Town of Wilbraham assembled in Town meeting on ye 20th of July instant A. D. 1772.

Gentlemen, the subscriber desires audience in the name and behalf of those in the South part of the Town of Wilbraham who have petitioned said Town to consent that they (with others included within ye limits petitioned for) be incorporated into a Town and have ye priviledges by law allowed such a body. While he shall honestly tho' breafly give ye reason for such desire, with the incouragement your humble petitioners have to seek such a priviledge. And as to our Reasons for desiring such a priviledge for ourselves, 'tis not any dissatisfaction with our Rev. Pastors, or offence taken with ye ccb or authority of ye Town, no Private Piques, grudge, or ill will at any; but purely that we & our Families may enjoy a preached Gospel which we esteem among ye greatest of priviledges; our distance from meeting is so great, ye season for a great part of ye year difficult & we so unable to Keep Horses & Furniture, that it is truly ye Case that for ye greatest part of our Families are obliged to stay at home. We have several hundred souls within ye Limits petitioned for & but a small part of them do or can attend public worship. And well knowing what a tendency staying from Public Worship has to indispose people thereto; and make them easy without it & yet how much depends thereon, as 'tis the appointed means of Salvation, 'tis a continual greaf to us that so many in our families are obliged to stay at home on Sabbath days, & our great fear is that by this means they forgit Sabbath Sanctification, & grow cold to ye Worship of God. This is our principle motive & we doubt not but you our Fathers will think it laudable and will feel a tender concern for us and our poor Families while under those circumstances. But we doubt not your Paternal Care for us, yet we fear yt you will think yt our poverty forbids us to think of Supporting ye Gospel & you to incourage us in such an undertaking. We beg leave therefore to inform you, for your incouragement & our own yt we have 47 Families within ye Limits asked for, as less numbers have sometimes supported ye Gospel — and when a people honestly venter for ye Cause of Religion we believe they may Expect a blessing. Further we have 20 young men Rated among us — a great deal of unimproved land yt is in itself capable of profitable Improvement. This incouragement we have Exclusive of Wales (as 'tis called) which borden upon us & we are in hopes may be annexed to us, which will be a very considerable help. If you our Fathers should object yt our want of union in ye principles of Religion is to you discouraging, we would say yt we know yt unity is ye strength & beauty of a People & we desire nothing more than to be one in Faith and Profession, in Love practice and consecration & Wherein this is not ye case we do truly

Lament it, & are fixedly determined to study ye things yt make for peace and whereby we may edify one another — But we pray it may be Remembered yt at this day most Towns and Societies have malecontents in them, yt we in this are not singular. Further it deserves to be considered whether we are not more Likly to have peace (& upon good grounds too) while we are in a Laudable way striving to advance ye peaceful Kingdom of ye Redeemer, amongst us, than we should be to sit still? We cannot but hope yt ye setting up of ye Gospel among us & building ye House of God in this place will happily make us of one heart and one way! yt with one mouth we may glorify God — Thus Fathers, we have briefly given you our reasons and incouragements which we pray you duly to consider, & we doubt not but you will favour your humble petitioners in ye thing for which we continue to pray as in duty bound. ASA CHAFFEE in the name and behalf of others.

Note " B."

The first announcement made for preaching and building the meeting-house was made January 29, 1783, and was as follows:

To the Committee for the South Parish in Wilbraham.

These may certify that the subscribers have assessed the Polls and Estates of the Inhabitants of the South Parish in Wilbraham in the sums hereafter named and have committed them to Zadok Stebbins and Daniel Carpenter, Constables, with warrant to collect the same, and have ordered them to pay the same to John Bliss Esq Treasurer for sd Parish by the first day of March next — viz

To hire Preaching in sd Parish in the sum of . . . . £20. 7. 8.
For Building Meeting House in sd Parish ye sum of . 103 1. 3

£123. 8. 11.

Wilbraham, January 29, 1783.

NOAH STEBBINS
ENOCH BURT
THO' KING
Assessors of the South Parish in Wilbraham.

Note " C."

Wilbraham June 9, 1783.

We the subscribers for value Received promis to pay Comfort Chaffee for & in behalf of the South Parish of Wilbraham the sum of four pounds Ten shillings on Demand with interest till paid witness our hands,

DAVID BURT,
ROBERT SESSIONS,
THOS KING,
LEWIS LANGDON.

Note " D."

To Zadok Stebbins, Constable,

Sir, Please Pay Lieut Noah Stebbins and Lieut Thomas King and Moses Stebbins or either of them, a committee to hire preaching in the South Parish of Wilbraham, the sum of five pounds nine shillings and eight pence and this shall discharge you so much of the Ministers Rate committed to you to collect, £5.-9-8

JOHN BLISS, Parish Treasurer

Wilbraham Jany 12th, 1784.

Wilbraham, March 1st, 1784.

To Daniel Carpenter, Constable, Sir, Bepleased to pay Lieut Saml Sexton and Capt Paul Langdon, a committee to Hire Preaching, four Pounds six shillings & nine pence two farthings and this Recipt shall discharge you so much of the Ministers Rate committed to you to collect.   JOHN BLISS Treasurer.

Note " E."

To Stephen Stebbins, Constable, Sir, be pleased to pay to the several persons the sums affixed to their names, viz.

To David Burt	£1: 10:	0
To Calvin Stebbins.	1: 0:	0
To Asa Chaffee	0: 12:	0
To Comfort Chaffee	0: 14:	0
To Abner Chapin	0: 1:	3
To David Burt, Lewis Langdon, Thomas King, Robert Sessions and Asa Chaffee, the committee for superintending the building the meeting House, the sum of	6: 7. 4:	2

                                              £10: 10. 7. 2

And this Receipt shall Discharge you so much
                                    JOHN BLISS, Parish Treasurer
Wilbraham Mhch 19, 1784.

Legal meeting of the South Parish in Wilbraham March 28, 1786. Voted and Granted to Capt. Paul Langdon and Lieut Samll Sexton six shillings for carrying Grain to Springfield in pay for Preaching.

Legal meeting of the South Parish in Wilbraham April 9. 1787. Voted and Granted to Lieut Samll Sexton Three shillings for going after preacher.
                          Attest MOSES STEBBINS JUNR Clerk
Wilbraham Nov. 21st 1787.

Note " F."

Occasionally the treasurer of the parish was obliged to borrow money, and generally by giving his note, as in the following instance:
                                    Wilbraham, October 25, 1784.

I for value Recd of Edward Morris for the use of the South Parish in Wilbraham the sum of Four Pounds Lawful silver money, which sum I promise for myself and successor in the office of Treasurer of the South Parish in Wilbraham to Pay to said Edward Morris or his order on demand with interest till as witness my hand,
                                    DAVID BURT, Treasurer.

Note " G."

The following named persons were members of the church at the ordination of Mr. Warren — sixty-five in number:

Sarah Abbe,	Enoch Burt,
John Bliss.	Joseph Bumpstead,
Abial (Colton) Bliss,	Ruth Beebe (probably wife of
David Burt,	Samuel),

Joel Chaffee,
John Chaffee,
Mehitable (Mascraft) Chaffee,
Simeon Chaffee,
Love (Davis) Chaffee,
Jonathan Chaffee,
Hepzibah Chaffee,
Olive Chaffee, wife of Jonathan,
Mehitable Chaffee, 2d,
Rowland Crocker,
Miriam Crocker,
Elizabeth Chapin,
Thomas Davis,
Sarah Davis,
John Firmin,
Rebecca Hutchinson,
John Hitchcock,
Thankful (Burt) Hitchcock,
Lucy (King) Jones, wife of Isaac,
William King,
Abigail King.
Eunice King,
Paul Langdon,
Thankful (Stebbins) Langdon,
John Langdon,
Thomas Lewis,
Mary Lewis,
Sarah Morris, widow of Isaac,
Darius Morris,

Edward Morris,
Lucy (Bliss) Morris,
Joseph Mason,
Timothy Patterson,
Elizabeth Patterson,
Mary Palmer,
Ezekiel Russell.
Tabitha (Flint) Russell,
Hannah Russell. wife of Ezekiel
  Russell, Jr.,
Samuel Sexton,
Sarah Sexton,
William Stacy,
Anna Stacy, wife of William,
Aaron Stebbins,
Moses Stebbins,
Hannah (Hale) Stebbins, wife of
  Moses, Jun.,
Moses Stebbins, Jun.,
Esther Stebbins, daughter of
  Moses,
Noah Stebbins,
Margaret Stebbins, wife of
  Noah,
Eldad Stebbins,
Anna Stebbins, wife of Eldad,
Zadok Stebbins,
Elizabeth (Pease) Stebbins. wife
  of Zadok.

Note " H."

DEACON HITCHCOCK.

Deacon John Hitchcock was the son of John Hitchcock of Springfield, and was born April 21, 1722. He was a descendant of Luke Hitchcock, an early settler of Wethersfield, who came from Fenny Compton, County of Essex, Eng.

Deacon Hitchcock married Thankful Burt, May, 1743. He was a soldier in the Revolution, serving at the time of the Lexington Alarm and afterwards in Captain Warriner's company, at Saratoga. His wife died July 17, 1800. He died October 11, 1807. He possessed great physical strength. It was said of him that he could outrun a horse, turn over a haycart, and lift a load of hay. He had a double row of teeth, sound at the time of his death. He could hold a tenpenny nail and break it off with his teeth. He said he did not know a man he could not whip *or run away from.*

Note ' I.'

There is more light on this matter than Dr. Stebbins supposed. The fact was that it was brought in some way before the Southern Association of Ministers, the record of which is as follows:

The Southern Association of Ministers, in the County of Hampshire, being convened at the house of the Rev. Ebenezer Gay, D.D., on Tuesday, Oct. 14, 1794, Mr. John Williams, member of the Church of Christ in the South Parish of Wilbraham. appeared before the association requesting their opinion in certain matters of difficulty be-

tween him and said church. From authentic documents it appeared that all matters had been previously considered by a mutual council which resulted in his favor. After attending to the matter the association are free in the opinion that the church ought to receive Mr. Williams to their friendly communion upon that result of council, and that they have acted an inconsistent part in first voting to forgive their brother and then revoking their forgiveness. The association further observe that they are willing to admit Mr. Williams to communion in their respective churches should opportunity occasionally present.   EBENEZER GAY, Moderator.
    Suffield, Oct. 14th, 1794.   J. F. M.

    While the matter of Mr. Williams' standing in the church was pending, he entered a complaint against Elisha Woodward, the keeper of the village store.

To the Honourable John Bliss, Esq., one of the Justices of the Peace
    for the County of Hampshire.
                        Hampshire, s.s.
    John Williams, of Wilbraham, in said county yeoman, complains and informs your Honour that Elisha Woodward of said Wilbraham, Shop Keeper, on the Eighth day of Jany instant did utter profane oaths or curses, one of them to the following effect, " The infernal cuss, John Williams I mean, if I had him out of the New England states, by G—d I would horse whip him," all which is contrary to Law and against the Peace of this Commonwealth. Your complainant therefore prays your Honour to issue your warrant to the apprehending of the said Elisha, that he may be tried before yourself or some other Justice of the Peace that he may be made to do and suffer as to Law and justice appertains and your complainant as in duty bound shall ever pray.   JOHN WILLIAMS.
    Wilbraham 8th of January 1794.

    The writ was issued and served by Jonathan Chaffee, constable, and Comfort Chaffee, Thomas King, and Lieutenant Jonathan Chaffee were summoned to appear and give evidence.
    Mr. Williams' efforts in sustaining order did not end with the trial of Mr. Woodward. A few weeks later he entered the following complaint:

To John Bliss Esq one of the Justices of the Peace in and for the
    County of Hampshire and Commonwealth of Massachusetts.
    John Williams of Wilbraham, in sd county, yeoman, complains in behalf of the Commonwealth and gives your Honor to be informed that Phœbe Barton of Wilbraham in sd county, spinster, at sd Wilbraham, on the ninth day of March last past, being Lords Day, did with force and arms within the walls of a House of Public Worship then and there behave rudely and indecently to the great disturbance of your complainant and divers good subjects of the Commonwealth and their statutes in such case made and provided — wherefore your complainant prays the sd Phœbe may be brought before your Honor to answer to the sd complaint and be dealt with as to Law and Justice appertains.   JOHN WILLIAMS.
    Wilbraham 10th of April 1794.

    The writ was issued, Phœbe was summoned to appear before a Justice of the Peace to answer the complaint, and Lydia Willey, Frank Patterson, and Fanny Chaffee summoned as witnesses. The result does not appear.   J. F. M.

Note " J."

Contract for finishing the meeting-house:

Wilbraham 20th November 1791.

We the subscribers jointly and severally obligate ourselves and stand firmly Bound by these present unto Comfort Chaffee, Steward Beebe, Robert Sessions, Stephen West, and David Burt, the sd Parish Committee for the consideration of two hundred forty-six pounds fifteen shillings to finish and complete the Meeting house in sd Parish (except glazing) in the following manner. To furnish materials, and clabboard the outside with good white Pine quarter boards, in a proper manner, suitable, with not exposing the clabboards more than 3½ Inches with a proper Coating at each side and turned at each corner, likewise outside to be painted the Body of it, thus with three coats, the first time with three quarters of it with Spanish white and the rest white lead mixed with good linseed oil. The Roof to be painted twice with Spanish brown mixed with linseed oil. The Inside thus with a Pulpit and Canopy equal in goodness with those of Somers Meeting House, and the walls to be sealed around as high as the windows and lathed and plastered above the seating, to make in the lower part twenty nine pews with raising on the ground on the walls eight inches and Body five inches, to make two pair of stairs with stair case with six pillars to support the Galleries, to make as many pews by the walls of the Galleries as is convenient equal to those of Somers M. house, Pew ground to be of suitable hight and the remainder of the galleries to be filled with seats as many as maybe with a decent brest work before the galleries to paint sd pulpit Canopy brest work and pillars of sd house common to such purpose in such buildings equal to Summors M. house, to seal the walls of sd galleries up to the windows and lath and plaster all above and overhead including under galleries with whitewashing the same. Every Branch of sd house to be completed in a workmanlike manner as wainscotting &c suitable for such buildings with plainness and neatness.

The contents of this Instrument comprehends finishing sd house (except glazing) to the turn of the Key all with simplicity and neatness the whole to be completed in twelve Months from Date.

Witness our hands

Witnesses, { AARON STEBBINS, ELISHA WOODWARD, JASON DOWNER, ICHABOD BLISS,

REV. MOSES WARREN.

Mr. Warren married Lydia, daughter of Colonel John Bliss. The exact date of the marriage is not of record, but the intention of marriage was published September 8, 1788. Their children were: Moses, born January 10, 1790, was graduated at Williams College in 1811: he went South, and died near New Orleans at the age of thirty-six. Lydia, born April 18, 1792; married Rev. Levi Smith. She died September 5, 1875. John Bliss Warren, born May 20, 1794, was graduated at Brown University in 1815. He studied for the ministry. He went to the South. For several years he was a missionary of the Presbyterian Church in Mobile. He afterwards preached in Louisiana, and, subsequently, established a school or college near New Orleans. He established the first Protestant paper in Louisiana. Aaron Warren, born May 30, 1794, died May 19, 1851. He was a farmer. He married Elizabeth Stacy.

8

A few anecdotes of Mr. Warren are extant. On one occasion he exchanged with the minister at Somers, Conn. It was on the Sunday before Thanksgiving. Mr. Warren read the proclamation of the Connecticut governor, and then, unmindful of locality, he uttered the benediction which he was accustomed to use at home, "God save the Commonwealth of *Massachusetts*."

Mr. Warren's family government was of a mild kind. The rod, so prevalent in his time, was seldom used by him, and the lack of the use of it sometimes brought cases of disobedience. He one day entertained a neighboring minister, and attempted to do so in the customary way. "John," said he to one of his boys, "take a pitcher and go down cellar and draw some cider." "I won't," said John. Turning to his guest to apologize for John's behavior, he said: "John is a very good boy generally, but he has a bad cold just now." It is to be presumed that the guest did not go away without the cider. John recovered from his cold in due time. He became obedient to a higher command, and entered the gospel ministry.

COLONEL JOHN BLISS.

Thomas Bliss, a native of Belstone, Devonshire, Eng., who was born probably between the years 1580 and 1585, came to Boston in 1635. He removed to Hartford before 1639, and with his oldest son Thomas settled on land in the vicinity of the present Lafayette and Oak streets, directly south of the present State Capitol grounds. He had five sons and four daughters. He died in 1640. Thomas, the son, removed to Saybrook and from there to Norwich. His widow, Margaret (whose maiden name is supposed to have been Lawrence), with her sons, Nathaniel, Lawrence, Samuel, and John, removed to Springfield in 1643, where she died August 28, 1684, aged ninety.

Nathaniel Bliss, the second son, married Catherine, daughter of Deacon Samuel Chapin of Springfield. He died November 8, 1654. He had four children: Samuel, born November 7, 1647; Margaret, born November 12, 1649, died April, 1745, aged ninety-six; Mary, born September 23, 1651; Nathaniel, born March 27, 1653, died December 23, 1736, aged eighty-three.

Widow Catherine Bliss married 2d, Thomas Gilbert, and had four children. Thomas Gilbert died in 1662, and she again married in 1664 Samuel Marshfield, and had four children. She died in 1712. Samuel Bliss, son of Nathaniel, married July 2, 1672, Sarah Stebbins, daughter of Lieutenant Thomas Stebbins, Springfield, who was born in England in 1620, and died in 1683. Sarah Stebbins was born in 1654, and died in 1726. They had nine children, Samuel, Nathaniel, Sarah, Margaret, Thomas, Hannah, John, Samuel, and Ebenezer.

Samuel Bliss lived in Longmeadow. He died June 19, 1739, aged nearly one hundred and two years, and was said to have nine children, thirty-eight grandchildren, one hundred and fourteen great-grandchildren, and ten great, great grandchildren. He was said to have possessed great physical strength. The story is told of him he caught a deer while swimming in the Connecticut River, and held its head under the water until it was drowned.

John Bliss, fourth son of Samuel, married Lydia Pease of Sunderland. He died in Longmeadow, October 8, 1784, nearly ninety-four. His wife died February 29, 1760, aged sixty-five. They had two children:

John, born February 1, 1727.

Aaron, born May 3, 1730, died February 1, 1810; aged eighty.

Colonel John Bliss married November 8, 1749, Abiel, daughter of Josiah and Margaret (Pease) Colton. She was a descendant of " Quartermaster " George Colton, one of the early settlers of Springfield and the first planter in Longmeadow. In 1747 he bought lots 117 and 118 in the " Fourth Precinct," and about 1750 he settled on this land, which lay on the " middle road," south of the Scantic River, about three-fourths of a mile up the hill. To this he made subsequent additions. He was a farmer and trader. He was a self-taught man, possessed of high native talents, and was a man of great influence. He was a soldier in the French war. In 1773 he was chosen to represent the district in the General Court, and again the next year, the last Provincial General Court. He was an ardent whig in the Revolution.

He was chosen to the three Provincial Congresses, and served on important committees. On the 8th of April, 1775, he was sent as commissioner to Connecticut to request that colony to co-operate with Massachusetts in the raising and establishing an army for the general defense. After the battle of Lexington he was sent again. He continued to be a representative until the adoption of the Constitution in 1780. He had held the office of major, and February 8, 1776, was appointed lieutenant-colonel in the militia. October 7, 1777, he was appointed colonel of the first Hampshire County regiment. He served some time in Westchester County. He was the only field officer which Wilbraham furnished during the war. He was chosen to the Senate under the first Constitution, and several times re-elected. In 1786 he was chosen executive councillor. He had early been appointed a justice of the peace by the House of Representatives and Council before the adoption of the Constitution. He was appointed by Governor Hancock a judge of the Court of Common Pleas. In person, Colonel Bliss was tall and spare and of light complexion. His wife was short and of light complexion. She died September 30, 1803. They had the following children:

Oliver, born September 15, 1751, died January 13, 1756; aged six years.

Lydia, born May 9, 1752, died June 29, 1755, and was the first person buried in the burial ground in South Wilbraham.

Lydia, born June 19, 1756; married Rev. Moses Warren.

Abiel, b. June 1, 1758; m. Josiah Cooley of Longmeadow.

Lucy, b. March 1, 1761, d. March 31, same month.

Lucy, b. March 28, 1762; m. Edward Morris March 28, 1782.

Mrs. Bliss died September 30, 1803. A year afterward, September 10, 1804, Colonel Bliss married Mrs. Sarah (Chaffee) Morris, widow of Isaac Morris and mother of Edward Morris, who had married his daughter Lucy twenty-one years before. He was then in his seventy-seventh year, and she in her seventy-sixth. He died November 8, 1809, aged nearly eighty-three. Mrs. Bliss survived him nearly nine years, and died April 21, 1818, aged eighty-nine.

BURT FAMILY.

Henry Burt, the ancestor of the Burt family, was first in Roxbury. In 1640 he removed to Springfield, where he was appointed clerk of the writs, or town clerk. He died April 30, 1662. His wife's name was Ulalia. She died August 29, 1690. They had ten children, two sons and eight daughters. The sons were Jonathan and Nathaniel.

Nathaniel married Rebecca Sykes, Jan. 15, 1662. They had eight children, of whom David, born in 1668, died July 5, 1735, married Martha Hale of Enfield, January 27, 1706. They had five children, of whom Captain David, born August 20, 1709, died July 5, 1735, married Sarah Colton, September 5, 1732. They had twelve children, of whom were:

David, b. November 5, 1736, d. July 6, 1809.

Enoch, b. October 3, 1742, died March 29, 1809, both of whom settled in South Wilbraham and became members of the church.

David Burt married Mary Colton, March 1, 1758. They had:

Solomon, b. February 1, 1759, d. May 7, 1777; Calvin, b. September 14, 1761; Flavia, b. March 12, 1764, d. 1787, m. —— Field; Abigail, b. April 27, 1767, m. Zebulon Betts of Richmond; Mary, b. June 18, 1769, m. Eliakim Williams; Jerusha, b. November 11, 1771, d. January 20, 1775; Sarah, b. January 27, 1774, m. William Williams; Jerusha, b. January 20, 1782, m. Rev. Hubbell Loomis.

Enoch Burt married Eunice Stebbins, November 28, 1766. They had Walter, b. October 20, 1767; Eunice, b. July 18, 1770; Enoch, b. ——. Eunice the mother died May 7, 1786, and Enoch the father married again, Mary Stacy, who died in childbirth. He married again, Thankful Skinner of Woodstock, and had Calvin, b. November 10, 1780; Lathrop, b. April 11, 1782; William, b. May 26, 1784.

THE CHAFFEE FAMILY.

Thomas Chaffee, who was at Hingham in 1637, was the ancestor of the Chaffee family. In 1660 he removed to Swansea. He had two sons, Nathaniel and Joseph, the dates of whose births are not known.

Joseph Chaffee married Anne Martin of Rehoboth. They had two sons and five daughters, of whom

John Chaffee, b. September 16, 1673, married Sarah Hills of Malden, July 17, 1700. They had five sons:

Joel Chaffee, b. 1702, d. June 20, 1745, unmarried.

Ebenezer Chaffee, b. September 22, 1704.

Joseph Chaffee, b. January 17, 1706.

Hezekiah Chaffee, b. April 19, 1708, d. October 27, 1730.

John Chaffee, b. February 10, 1707, m. Mehitable Mascroft, April 14, 1730.

Mrs. Sarah Chaffee died at Woodstock April 17, 1735. John Chaffee (the father) then married, in September or October, 1735, Elizabeth Hayward. He died December 2, 1757, aged eighty-five. Mrs. Elizabeth Chaffee died February 5, 1760, aged eighty-seven. Joseph Chaffee married Hannah May, daughter of Ephraim May of Rehoboth. He removed from Barrington to Woodstock in 1729. He settled in West Woodstock. He filled various offices in Woodstock, was influential in the meetings of that parish, and the establishing of the church. About 1754 he removed to Wilbraham (then Springfield) and settled in the district of "Wales." His farm extended from Ball Mountain to the Brimfield (Mass.) line. He died of small-pox March 15, 1760. His widow married Ensign Joseph Sexton, and died May 26, 1784, in her eighty-fourth year. They had:

Sarah, b. June 18, 1729, in Barrington.

Joseph, b. January 9, 1731, in Woodstock.

Benjamin, b. July 10, 1732.

Ephraim, b. 1733.

Asa, b. June 5, 1734.

Jonathan, b. March 11, 1735-6, d. July 21, 1737.

Comfort, b. March 20, 1737-8.

Isaiah, b. April 5, 1740.

Hannah, b. June 7, 1742.

Darius, b. May 13, 1744.

Joel, b. February 16, 1746.

Joseph Chaffee, first son of Joseph, b. January 9, 1731, married Esther Chaffee. He is said to have died in Union, Conn. They had a daughter, Anne, b. May 6, 1776.

Benjamin Chaffee, second son of Joseph, b. July 10, 1732, married Hannah Skinner of Woodstock. They removed there. She died in 1811.

Ephraim Chaffee, third son of Joseph, b. ——, 1733, married Anna Torrey of Woodstock. He was killed by Indians at Lake George in 1757. They had a daughter, Sarah, b. March 26, 1758.

Isaiah Chaffee, seventh son of Joseph, married Betsy Manning, March 5, 1752.

Darius Chaffee, eighth son of Joseph, married Molly Chaffee, November 11, 1775. They had Henry, b. November 16, 1776.

Simeon Chaffee, son of Joel, married Love Davis of Somers; published October 19, 1765. They had:

Locea, b. October 2, 1766.

Simeon, b. September 10, 1776.

Noah, b. October 30, 1778.

Simeon Chaffee, died April 13, 1824, aged eighty-eight.

Asa Chaffee, fourth son of Joseph, married Mary Howlett of Woodstock, September 5, 1753. They had:

Jonathan, b. 1754.

Wesley, b. January 29, 1756.

Cerrel, b. May 19, 1758.

Ephraim, b. August 12, 1760.

Martha, b. May 18, 1761, d. June 29, 1762.

Luther, b. October 10, 1764.

Calvin, b. June 11, 1766.

Miriam, b. September 13, 1768.

Jemima, b. September 13, 1770.

Abiathar, b. December 5, 1774.

Walter, b. August 7, 1775.

Comfort Chaffee, sixth son of Joseph, married Mary, daughter of Nathaniel Bliss. They had:

Lucretia, b. June 27, 1760.

Mary, b. April 8, 1758.

Bathsheba, b. June 19, 1762, married Stephen West.

Mary, b. June 29, 1765.

Joel, b. September 27, 1770.

Nathaniel Bliss, b. December 14, 1772.

Comfort Chaffee died June 14, 1811.

WILLIAM KING.

William King came to Wilbraham from Springfield. He settled in the South Parish, on the spot where the Congregational Church now stands. He made his first purchase of land in 1744, and continued the purchase of adjoining land until he became one of the largest, if not the largest, land-owners in the south part of the town. He sold to the parish the land on which the meeting-house was built. He married Jemima Bliss, June 11, 1742. They had:

, William, b.

Thomas, b.

Solomon, b. February 7, 1748.

Jemima, b. July 4, 1750.

Lucy, b. Nov. 19, 1752, married Isaac Jones.

Luther, b. March 22, 1755.

Louisa, b. December 7, 1756, died September, 1758.

Walter, b. November, 1758.

Hosea, b. March 28, 1761.

At the outbreak of the Revolution he served as lieutenant at the Lexington Alarm. He was one of the town committee of correspondence and safety. His son Solomon entered the army and died in 1775. Mr. King sold his property to Jonathan Dwight of Springfield, April 7, 1784. Dwight sold it to Jason Downer in 1791. In 1793 Downer sold it to James Utley, and in 1797 Utley sold it to Jonathan Flynt of Hardwick — the two exchanging properties. Jonathan Flynt also bought a privilege on the Scantic, just below the present bridge, and set up a fulling mill, which is believed to have been the first attempt at cloth manufacturing in Wilbraham. In 1807 he sold the mill property to his son Jonathan, and in 1809 sold his residence property to his son Levi, and removed to Monson, where he died in 1814.

William King, Jr., married Thankful ————. They had:

Lovice, b. December 22, 1767.

Elora, b. December 14, 1769.

Lucy, b. March 18, 1775.

Polly, b. November 23, 1776.

William, b. September 26, 1778.

Hepzibah, b. December 7, 1782.

Thankful, b. September 20, 1788.

Thomas King married Eunice Chaffee of Somers, December 18, 1772. They had:

Eunice, b. November 9, 1773.

Thomas, b. January 15, 1775.

Luther King, married Abigail Ainsworth, October 13, 1781.

THE LANGDON FAMILY.

The ancestor of the Langdon family was Phillip Langdon, a mariner, a native of Yorkshire, Eng., who settled in Boston. He married Mary ————. His children were: Phillip, b. ———— ————; Susanna, b. October 23, 1677; John, August 22, 1682; James, August 15, 1685; Samuel, December 22, 1687; Mary, March 24, 1690; Paul, September 12, 1693.

Phillip Langdon died December 4, 1697. His wife died February 14, 1717.

Lieutenant Paul Langdon, b. September 12, 1693. He married Mary Stacy of Salem, August 17, 1718. He came to Wilbraham from Salem in 1741. He died December 3, 1761. His children were:

Mary, b. August 20, 1719; Lewis, May 12, 1721; Hannah, February 22, 1723; Paul, December 16, 1725; John, June 21, 1728; Elizabeth, July 1, 1730; Anna, September 24, 1732.

Captain Paul Langdon, b. December 16, 1725, married Thankful Stebbins, May 5, 1757. He died June 23, 1804. His children were:

Samuel, b. May 10, 1758, d. February 29, 1822; Thankful, July 4, 1760, m. ———— Burt; Paul, August 18, 1764; Lovice, November 13, 1768, m. Joseph Wood of Monson; Mary, October 12, 1770, m. Jacob Wood; Walter, June 22, 1779.

John Langdon, b. January 21, 1728, married 1st, Sarah Stebbins,

February, 1755. She died July 22, 1755, aged twenty-one. One child, Sarah, b. July 12, 1755, m. Ebenezer Crocker of Kinderhook, N. Y. Married 2d, Eunice Torrey of Mansfield, Conn., December 25, 1757. Their children were: John Wilson, b. March 11, 1759, m. Lucy Ashley; James, March 27, 1752, m. Esther Stebbins; Josiah, January 13, 1765, m. Sally Hall; Joanna, June 21, 1767, m. ———— Leonard, she died in Kentucky; Oliver, October 9, 1769, m. Catherine Bennett; Eunice, March 7, 1772, m. Asa Minitt; Solomon, July 19, 1773, m. Mary Butler; Artemas, May 25, d. October 2, 1760.

THE MORRIS FAMILY.

Edward Morris, the ancestor of this family, was born at Waltham Abbey, County of Essex, Eng., in 1630, and was brought to America probably before 1638. He is believed to have been the son of Thomas Morris, who died at Boston that year.

Edward Morris married Grace Bett, November 20, 1655. He was for twelve years selectman of Roxbury, and for nine years represented the town in the General Court. On the abolition of the colonial government and the suspension of the House of Representatives in 1686, he led a number of the Roxbury people in the settlement of Woodstock. In 1689 he was chosen selectman of the town and also appointed lieutenant, and thus became the leading military authority of the town, and died at the close of the year.

His son Edward, born in Roxbury in March, 1659, and was baptized by Rev. John Eliot, March 13 of that year. He married Elizabeth Bowen, May 24, 1683. After the death of his father he removed to Woodstock, where he died August 29, 1727. His wife survived him and died November 20, 1743. He was selectman of Woodstock for twenty-four years, and for twenty-two years deacon of the church. His son, Lieutenant Edward Morris, was born at Roxbury, November 9, 1688, and was baptized by Rev. Nehemiah Walter. He married, January 12, 1715, Bethiah Peake. He held various town offices and for nine years was selectman. He died August 12, 1769.

His son, Isaac Morris, was born in Woodstock, March 26, 1725. His intended marriage with Sarah Chaffee was published October 18, 1748. She was born January 18, 1729, and was the only daughter of Joseph and Hannah (May) Chaffee of Barrington, but at this time were residents of Woodstock. In 1761 Isaac Morris removed to Wilbraham (then Springfield) and settled in that part of the town then called "Wales," and near his father-in-law, Joseph Chaffee, who had preceded him some five or six years. His farm occupied what has been known as "Tray Hollow," on the road to Monson, which was laid out through his farm. While in Woodstock he held various parish offices. The records of the Woodstock church being lost, we have no date of his admission to the church. His wife joined the church in West Woodstock, April 30, 1750. He died January 10, 1778, after a long illness. His wife, after a widowhood of twenty-six years, married Hon. John Bliss, September 10, 1804. She survived him and was a second time a widow. She died April 27, 1818, aged eighty-nine. The children of Isaac and Sarah Morris were:

Hannah, b. January 13, 1750, in Woodstock.

Darius, b. September 15, 1751, in Woodstock.

Isaac, b. September 16, 1753, in Woodstock.

Joseph, b. March —, 1755, in Woodstock.

Edward, b. December 12, 1756, in Woodstock.

Elizabeth, b. July 10, 1759, in Woodstock; died at "Wales," March 24, 1764.

Sarah, b. July 20, 1761, in Woodstock; m. Stephen Pease of Somers.
Eunice, b. May 13, 1763, in " Wales."
Chester, b. April 16, 1765, in " Wales."
Ebenezer, b. March 15, 1767, in " Wales."
Elizabeth, b. February 17, 1769, in "Wales."
Ephraim, b. March 17, 1772, in " Wales."

Hannah married John Davis. She died August 18, 1825. Her children were: Roxanna, married Richard Firmin; Betsey, who also married Richard Firmin; Joseph, John, Asa, Sally.

Darius Morris married 1st, Elizabeth Fisher of East Haddam; married 2d, Rebecca Chandler of Woodstock. She died August 13, 1835, aged seventy-eight. Children:

By Elizabeth: Sylvester, b. August 4, 1775; Asenath, b. August 27, 1777, m. Henry Cady, removed to Butternuts, N. Y.

By Rebecca: Betsey, b. August 13, 1780, m. Dr. Isaac Wood; Joseph, b. February 27, 1782; Rebecca, b. January 21, 1784, m. Jesse Merwin; Darius, b. March 18, 1786, d. July 10, 1786; Fanny C., b. April 27, 1787, m. Elisha Bowen, Reading, Vt.; Sylinda, b. August 19, 1789, m. Noah Merwin; Hannah, b. July 6, 1791, m. James Adams; Sarah, b. June 21, 1793, m. Increase Clapp.

Isaac Morris married Irene Johnson of Stafford. He died June 26, 1805. His wife died May 14, 1842. Their children were:

Polly, b. December 19, 1781, m. Roswell Davis of Stafford; Sally, b. 1787, married John Hitchcock of Monson; Eunice, b. August 4, 1786, m. Alban Comstock of Westfield; Isaac, b. April 8, 1792; Irene, May 19, 1793, m. Arnon Comstock of Westfield; Roxana, b. June 22, 1795, m. Joel Hitchcock of Monson.

Edward Morris, b. December 12, 1756, m. Lucy, daughter of Hon. John Bliss. He died April 29, 1801. She died April 15, 1836. Children:

Oliver Bliss, b. September 22, 1782; Edward, b. July 21, 1784; Isaac, b. August 2, 1786; John Bliss, b. July 15, 1789; Lucy, b. February 23, 1791, m. Dr. D. Ufford; Abby Morris, b. March 10, 1793, m. Ralph R. Rollo, South Windsor, Conn.; Eliza, b. April 26, 1795, d. June 17, 1802; Richard Darius, b. August 30, 1797; Lydia, b. March 20, 1797, d. December 9, 1887; Edward Alonzo, b. March 14, 1801, d. 1858.

Eunice Morris, b. May 13, 1763, m. Joshua Clark of Windsor, Mass. They had ten children, all born in Windsor.

Chester Morris married Betsey Wales of Brimfield. He removed to Rochester, Vt., about 1800, and subsequently to Malone, N. Y. They had twelve children.

Ebenezer Morris married Ryndia May of Holland, Mass. He died there December 23, 1831. She was born October 7, 1769, and died February 1, 1844. They had: Leonard M., b. January 10, 1790; Anna, b. October 14, 1794, m. Augustus Moore of Union; Laura, b. February 8, 1798, m. W. P. Sessions of Union.

Elizabeth Morris married David Hume of Windsor, Mass., September 3, 1788. They had eleven children.

Ephraim Morris married October 16, 1796, Pamela, daughter of Jesse Converse of Stafford, Conn. She was born February 23, 1777. They had: Sylvester, b. September 23, 1797; Amanda, b. September 20, 1799; Edward, b. September 15, 1801; Pamela, b. October 6, 1803, all born in Stafford; Jesse Converse, b. August 7, 1805, d. 1806; Jesse Converse, March 7, 1807; Molly Converse, November 27, 1809; Joseph Converse, February 24, 1812, d. 1813; Julia, b. March 14, 1814; Eliza, b. December 24, 1816; Joseph, b. February, 1819. These were all born in Vermont. He died at Bethel, Vt., October 7, 1852. His wife died February 2, 1846.

THE RUSSELL FAMILY.

Ezekiel Russell was born in Reading in 1721. He married Tabitha, daughter of Ebenezer and Tabitha (Burnap) Flint of Reading. He removed first to Ashford, Conn., thence to Wilbraham in 1759. He died January 3, 1802. Mrs. Russell was born May 18, 1721, and died June 4, 1805. They had the following children:

Ezekiel, b. 1753, married 1st, Susan Hills, 2d, Hannah Meacham of Somers.

Tabitha, b. 1755, married Nathan Stedman; by Hon. John Bliss.

Robert, b. June 2, 1757, d. December 9, 1836; married Lydia Beebe.

Benjamin, b. 1762, d. in the army in 1778.

Asa, b. 1765, married Thankful Foot, and removed to western New York.

SESSIONS FAMILY.

Although the Sessions family had no connection with the church at the time of its organization, or at the ordination of Mr. Warren, it has been so strongly connected with its subsequent history that it cannot fail to be recognized.

The emigrant ancestor of this family was Alexander Sessions, who came from Wantage in England as early as 1672, in which year he was married and settled in Andover, Mass. He had nine children, one of whom, Nathaniel, was born August 8, 1681. He settled in Pomfret, Conn., where he married, and died later in 1771, at the age of ninety-one. He was a farmer, and up to the age of eighty-eight had managed his affairs personally. At this age he became blind. After he was eighty he committed to memory the Psalms, the New Testament, and portions of the Old. He had seven sons, one of whom, Amasa, born about 1721, married Hannah Miller of Rehoboth, Mass. They had nine children. Of these Robert Sessions was born March 15, 1752, and died in Wilbraham, September 27, 1836, at the age of eighty-four years and six months. He married Anna Ruggles of Pomfret, April 16, 1778. She was descended from the Roxbury family of that name. She died November 22, 1838, aged eighty-two. At the time of the destruction of tea in Boston harbor, Mr. Sessions was living in Boston, and formed one of that celebrated "Tea Party." He subsequently served in the army during the Revolution. He came to Wilbraham about 1782. He had the following children:

Betsey, born May 7, 1779, in Pomfret; married 1st, Levi Flynt. He died in 1828, and she married 2d, William Burt. She died in 1853.

Charles, b. December 22, 1780, in Pomfret; married Clarissa Granger. They had no children.

Robert, b. Feb. 2, 1783, in Wilbraham; married Charlotte Metcalf. They had George M., Elizabeth, Oscar, Maria, Jesse, Joseph, and Horace.

George, b. December 16, 1784; married Eunice Mather of Tolland, Mass. They had: Alexander H., Juliet, Milton, Horace, William, George, Eunice, John Quincy. George Sessions died in Michigan.

Nancy, b. April 17, 1787; married Rodney Comstock; removed to Worthington, O. No children.

Celina, b. August 6, 1789; married Cyrus Newell of Longmeadow. They had: Samuel, Nelson, Horace, and Charles.

Francis, b. August 27, 1792; married Sophronia Metcalf. They had one son, Francis Charles, b. February 27, 1820. He lived at Columbus, O. He died in 1892, without children.

Horace, b. January 28, 1794. Graduated at Hamilton College, studied theology at Andover, became agent of the American Colonization Society, went to Liberia with one of the first colonies, and died at sea on his passage home; unmarried.

Martha Phipps, b. June 23, 1795; married John West, February 12, 1818. They had: John Ruggles, b. February 15, 1809; Martha Jane, b. February 14, 1821, married S. C. Spellman.

Robert Sessions, b. December 28, 1823. Lived and died at Dubuque, Ia.

Hannah Miller, b. January 6, 1797; married —— Chapin; no children.

Sumner, b. December 29, 1797; married Mary Wood. They had: Mary, Harriet, Frances, and Edward Payson.

William Vine, b. September 14, 1801; married Lydia Ames. He lived on the old homestead. His children were: Nancy, William R., b. December 3, 1835, and Lydia, who married Rev. Mr. Woodworth of Berlin, Conn.

All of the children of Robert Sessions, with the exception of the two who were born in Pomfret, were baptized by Mr. Warren, and all became members of the church.

STACY FAMILY.

William Stacy came to Wilbraham from Salem. He was born in 1716, and died March 9, 1800, aged eighty-four. He was probably a descendant of Henry Stacy of Salem, and son of William Stacy. He married 1st Mary ——, who died April 11, 1761. He had lived for some years at Greenwich, in New Jersey, where his three oldest children were born. His wife may have belonged to that vicinity. He married 2d, November 9, 1766, Anna ——, who was born in Warren, R. I., February 19, 1727, and who died December 19, 1808. Children:

Mary, b. May 11, 1744.
William, b. February 8, 1746.
Simeon, b. January 20, 1748.
Sarah, b. March 8, 1750, in Springfield (Wilbraham).
Ebenezer, b. October 1, 1752; married Mary Chaffee, January 10, 1783.
Elizabeth, b. October 29, 1755; died November 4, 1757.
Richard, b. July 17, 1758; died March 20, 1759.
   By second wife:
Mahlon, b. May 11, 1765.
Anna, b. 1767.
Ruby, b. June 9, 1769; died October 10, 1770.
Gilbert, b. November 3, 1770.
William Stacy, Jr., married Thankful ——.
Chauncey, b. August 16, 1770.
Zorah, b. February 13, 1772.
Jemima, b. Nov. 9, 1773.

THE STEBBINS FAMILY.

The genealogy of the Stebbins family may be found in the volume which contains the historical address of Dr. Rufus P. Stebbins, given at the centennial of the town of Wilbraham in 1863.

Of the members of the family connected with the church in the South Parish, Aaron Stebbins married Mary Wood, October 18, 1744. Their children were: Mary, b. June 10, 1748; Aaron, March 20, 1750; James, December 31, 1751, d. —— ——; Seth, September 6, 1754; Martha, February 15, 1757, d. ——, ——; James, October 6, 1760. This family removed to Vermont.

Moses Stebbins married Dorcas Hale, January 29, 1749. Their children were: Moses, b. May 3, 1750; Calvin, July 30, 1751; Esther, January 26, 1755; Ambrose, October 17, 1756; Dorcas, February 17, 1759, d. ——, ——; David, February 29, 1760; Timothy, April 17, 1762; Dorcas, August 2, 1765; Chester, January 23, 1769; Thankful, March 21, 1773.

Noah Stebbins married Margaret Stebbins, May 22, 1765. Their children were: Noah, b. February 12, 1766; Azariah, October 27, 1767; Margaret, May 5, 1769; Elijah, January 14, 1772; Luther, October 25, 1773; Mary, December 8, 1775; Luther, June 12, 1777; John, August 13, 1779; Charity, November 23, 1781; Persis, September 23, 1784.

Eldad Stebbins married Ann Badger, April 11, 1765. Their children were: Ann, b. February 4, 1764; Bina, August 11, 1765; Eldad, June 13, 1767, d. ——, ——; Gilbert, March 11, 1769; Luther and Calvin, March 2, 1771, d. ——, ——; Lovice, March 7, 1762, d. ——, ——; Eldad, April 4, 1774; Luther, September 29, 1776; Calvin, March 5, 1778; Alpheus, July 28, 1780; Lovice, December 7, 1782.

Zadok Stebbins married Elizabeth Pease, November 14, 1764. Their children: Zadok, b. April 2, 1765; Augusta, March 28, 1767; John, September 15, 1769; Flavia, November 30, 1771; Chauncey, August 13, 1774; Abigail, August 14, 1776.

Moses Stebbins, Jun., married Hannah Hale, 1776. Their children were: Clarissa, Warren, Asenath, Hannah, Milo, David, Dorcas, Flavel.

THE WEST FAMILY.

Francis West, the ancestor of this family, came from Salisbury, Eng., and settled in Duxbury. He married Margery Russ, February 27, 1639. He was a carpenter by occupation, and died January 2, 1692, leaving a small estate. From him the Wilbraham Wests are descended in the following line: Samuel, who married Triphosa Partridge, September 26, 1668. He died May 8, 1689, aged forty-six. His wife died November 1, 1701.

John West, born March 6, 1679, settled in Lebanon, Conn. He married Deborah ——, who died November 17, 1741.

Solomon West, born March 15, 1723, in Lebanon. He married Abigail Strong, October 10, 1743, and removed to Tolland. He died August 21, 1790, aged forty-eight. Mrs. West died August 12, 1807, aged sixty-seven.

Stephen West, born in Tolland, August 19, 1759. Removed to Wilbraham, where he married Bathsheba Chaffee, daughter of Comfort Chaffee, November 27, 1783. He died April 17, 1814. Mrs. West died at Tolland, Conn., April 22, 1851, aged eighty-nine. Mr. West was treasurer of the parish in 1793, and succeeded John Hitchcock as deacon. He had the following children:

Stephen Strong, b. September 22, 1784.

Bathsheba, b. August 24, 1786.

Solomon, b. August 10, 1788, d. June 10, 1790.

Solomon, b. February 19, 1791, d. December 24, 1793.

John, b. October 1, 1793, d. July 12, 1826.

Ralph, b. May 6, 1796, d. March 9, 1801.

Solomon Ralph, b. April 8, 1801, d. December 23, 1803.

A son born December 23, 1803, died the same day.

Stephen Strong West married Lucinda Humeston, April 27, 1809. They had:

Lucinda Humeston, b. October 29, 1809.

Strong, b. August 5, 1811, d. August 19, 1880.

Solomon, b. June 15, 1813, d. April 17, 1815.

Anna H., b. February 6, 1816, d. November 6, 1889.
Stephen Otis, b. May 21, 1818, d. June 1, 1890.
George Spencer, b. January 23, 1822, d. December 14, 1896.
Solomon, b. February 4, 1824, d. March 30, 1873.
John, b. September 6, 1828.
Nancy Flynt, b. April 1, 1833.
Joel, b. November 13, 1835, d. March 23, 1897, at Los Angeles, Cal.

WILLIAMS FAMILY.

John Williams was a descendant of Robert Williams, who settled at Roxbury in 1637. His son Samuel married Theoda Parke, daughter of William Parke, Roxbury, 1631. Their son, Rev. John Williams, was the noted Indian captive, taken at the burning of Deerfield. His son, Rev. Stephen Williams, born May 14, 1693, died June 10, 1782. He was settled minister at Longmeadow in 1716; married in 1718 Abigail, daughter of Rev. John Davenport of Stamford, Conn., and had eight children, of which John Williams, b. March 8, 1720, married January 22, 1747, Ann Colton. His father was a large land-owner in the south part of Wilbraham, a part of which he improved, and on which John Williams settled. This was on the middle road and near the line of Somers. They had the following children: Stephen, b. November 8, 1747, d. 1750; Ann, b. September 8, 1750, d. 1764; Abigail, b. May 18, 1751, d. 1779; Mary, b. March 28, 1753, m. Noah Chapin; Stephen, b. July 28, 1755; Sarah, b. October 19, 1757, d. 1758; John, b. April 22, 1761; Elizur, b. April 15, 1764.

Ann Williams, the mother, died November 23, 1771. The father was afterwards twice married, without more children. He died in April, 1791. His son, John Williams, was the person so long in controversy with the church. This whole family disappeared from the town.

WALES.

A gore of land lying to the northwest of Somers and southeast of Springfield, one mile in width at its eastern end and somewhat less at its western end, now comprises the extreme southern part of Hampden. Although within the jurisdiction of Massachusetts, it was not for some years included within the limits of any town and was known as the "District of Wales." At just what time this territory began to be settled it is difficult to state. Grants of land in this section were made by the General Court early in the last century. In July, 1728, two hundred acres were granted to Captain Thomas Colton of Springfield (Longmeadow). This land was laid out December 19, 1734, to Rev. Stephen Williams and Captain Isaac Colton, and is described as "ye land lying and being in yt Gore of Province Land in ye county of Hampshire yt is between Springfield on ye North and ye Colony or Patent line on ye South, Brimfield on ye east and Somers on ye west, in ye S. E. corner of sd land." May 22, 1735, two hundred acres were laid out to Nathaniel Collins. December 9, 1742, two hundred acres were laid out to Stephen Williams. February 17, 1744, one hundred and ninety-one acres were laid out to Ebenezer Jones, and subsequently more land was laid out to Stephen Williams. Jones is supposed to have settled on his grant, but afterwards conveyed it to Peter Tufts, whose heirs, Moses Tufts and others of Ashford, sold to Joseph Chaffee of Woodstock, December 6, 1751, who, on September 20, 1754, bought one hundred and fifty acres of Mr. Williams, and again on January 13, 1756, bought of him one hundred and fifty-five acres more, making all his holding about five hundred acres. He built his house on the spot since occupied by the Firmin family east of Pine Mountain. Henry Badger, from Union, settled near him, and these are supposed to have been among the earliest settlers in this section, the Skinners, Carpenters, and other families following. John Williams, son of Rev. Stephen Williams, settled in the central part of the tract, at the western foot of Bald Mountain, near the line of Somers. As the years rolled on and the population increased, the inhabitants were anxious for town privileges, and desired to be annexed to Wilbraham. At a town meeting held March 17, 1772, it was voted that the petition of Mr. John Williams and others requesting to be joined to and incorporated with Wilbraham be accepted with this restriction, viz., that the whole gore of land with the present Freeholders adjoining to Wilbraham from East to West the whole width of Wilbraham be annexed agreeable to said request exclusive of all others.